The best way to predict the future is to

. LINCOLN

CONTENTS

INTRODUCTION

"I keep getting charged off my bank for going overdrawn," I told him.

"It is a cycle. They charge me now when I am not overdrawn, which causes me to become overdrawn so they can repeat the process again next month".

My Dad shook his head and responded, "come on, we will go and talk to them".

My branch was on the high street and it was only a five-minute walk from his office, so we made our way over on foot. It was a Friday lunchtime, so the streets were busy with the city's work-force out on their breaks and enjoying the warm weather.

When we arrived at the bank, they had installed a new ticket system in which it required you to print out a ticket from the machine and then wait for them to call your number before you could speak with an employee.

Not caring for this system, however, my Dad just made his way up to the front of the bank.

"Excuse me sir, there are people ahead of you who have been waiting," one woman said without success.

It was like water off a ducks back as undisturbed he continued with his forward advance to the cashier sitting behind the glass at the front of the bank.

"You keep charging my son for going overdrawn," he exclaimed. "I want you to close his account today".

The cashier conscious there was a room full of onlooking customers, then echoed the sentiments of the disgruntled customer and advised that he would first require a ticket before she could speak with him.

What she encountered next was a level of savagery that she will never forget.

His choice of language was so profane and depraved that you cannot help but be impressed by the creativity to think up such a response.

He made it clear in no uncertain terms the account would be closed and he would not be getting a ticket from any machine.

The ferocious explosion back was so ruthless that it shocked the entire bank as the peripheral noise from those being served and the others still waiting came to an immediate stop.

It can be a harrowing experience to be on the wrong side of my Dad. When he shouts, it is with such vehement and anger that it will instil terror in even the most assured of people.

The words do not even need to be directed at you and yet you will still stop what you are doing and enter a heightened state of alertness.

"I cannot close the account in case there are future charges we still need to take," the nervous cashier uttered in response.

This appeared to enrage him more. He erupted back even louder and with even more expletives than before and again demanded that they close the account.

It was relaxing on the walk over from his office as we enjoyed the afternoon sun and chatted about nothing in particular, so I was as surprised as the cashier as he flipped between a state of Zen to psychotic rage in what seemed like a second.

Another bank employee then attempted to interject in the hope of defusing the situation. He was sat on one of the desks to the side of us, however as he got up he was told to sit back down with such threatening menace that he did not dare say another word.

The bank manager then stormed down from the back of the bank. She appeared to be just as confrontational as my Dad and she was shouting as she was making her way toward us.

Her tone was overflowing with disdain and she shouted back at what seemed like the top of her voice, "how dare you speak to my employees that way!".

I do not know if she thought her authority would calm the situation or if she was just acting on pure emotion, but it did not help. The look of terror that washed over her face was palpable

as my Dad began maiming her with his expansive vocabulary.

I looked around at the faces of the other customers in the bank and could see that they all looked terrified. It had taken on the feel of a hostage situation from a bank heist you witness during a movie.

As I was looking at all the terrified customers, I then noticed a face I recognised within the crowd.

The impending dread that would next consume me upon the realisation that he was someone who worked in my office was immediate. At the precise moment in my mind when the penny dropped as to where I recognised him from, I was mortified.

Talk about embarrassing...

My Dad has been like this all my life though. He is an enigma. Hilarious and charming as he is terrifying and formidable.

They closed the bank account for me that day, but not before some of the longest and most awkward few minutes of my life.

I vowed after that however that I would never allow myself to go overdrawn again, and if it ever happened, I would not let my Dad know about it for sure.

This was how my life was back then, though. I was always low on money and counting the days until pay day, but then when I would get paid it would be for such a paltry amount that in no

time at all I was broke again.

I knew I needed to make some drastic changes in my life.

For a start, I had to earn a much better annual income from my job, but I also needed to learn how to manage my money much better and stop spending it the moment I would receive it.

In this book, I will tell you my story.

After needing to leave school at only sixteen years old with no qualifications, I had to make my way in life from the bottom. Unable to save anything from my minimum wage salary, I was in constant debt.

Only a few months prior I had been told by my career advisor to accept my future, as that was all I would ever earn.

I told him I wanted to work with computers in the IT industry, but that made him chuckle with a condescending laugh.

"Nobody will hire you to work with computers," he said.

"I have found you a job working as a porter in a hotel. You will need to carry the guest's luggage to their rooms when they arrive. I have arranged for you to do your work experience with them for a week and if you do good, they might offer you a permanent job".

Not a chance.

Never settle, keep pushing. That will forever be my mantra.

Twenty years later and I am the Director of three companies. I am a property investor that owns and manages multiple properties and I am also a business consultant that has earned a six-figure annual income working with some of the most well-known and reputable companies in the world for coming up to a decade.

Prior to becoming a business consultant, I made my way from the bottom of the corporate ladder into ever-increasing senior positions within change management, taking on larger roles with more power and responsibility following each promotion.

Never let them write you off.

Over the coming pages, I will equip you with all the techniques you need to know so you can also take control of your future and get what you deserve from life.

WHO, WHAT AND WHY?

Chapter 1

I once read a quote that stated, "We lose ourselves in books and we can find ourselves there too," and I struggle to think of a better way to express the beauty of great literature other than the way of this quote.

Books can revolutionise how we view the world and live our lives.

It has been an ambition of mine to write a book for some time, but I could never decide on the subject. There are many great stories I have to share in an autobiography, but then who would want to read those when I am not already a well-known personality?

Perhaps I should create a great work of fiction I would question, full of suspense and twists with detailed character profiles that the reader can get invested into? My mind would flood with various back stories for each character and how their stories would intertwine with one another.

Then I would question, would that be the best use of my time and could I write something more meaningful?

So, after some deliberation of my life experiences, I have recalled the times in my life when I have most needed support and information along with the greatest lessons which I have learned along the way so I can share my experience to benefit others.

I am a confident person, but when making big life decisions my mind would fill with doubt and reservations. What felt like the greatest idea ever would shrink as the voices of those who doubted me would become louder than my inner optimism.

Self-confidence is a fundamental cornerstone to achieving the most we can in life, and it is a skill which we should not underestimate.

I expect that many great businesses never get off the ground because of the crippling doubts of those considering starting them up. I am also just as sure that many great people could do so much better in their careers, but the inner doubts that they are not good enough will restrict them.

While I have doubted myself, I have also been fortunate enough to have kept enough faith and confidence to craft the life I wanted without the fear of failure overruling my actions.

Steve Jobs once said,

"When you grow up you get told the world is the way it is and to live your life inside the world. Try not to bash into the walls too much. Try to have a nice family, have fun, save a little money. That's a very limited life. Life can be much broader once you discover one simple fact: Everything around you which you call life was made up by people that were no smarter than you and you can change it, you can influence it, you can build your own things that other people can use. Once you learn that, you will never be the same".

Despite its power, that quote alone will not convince you of your self-worth, but you will do well to remember it as over-time you will find more and more examples that confirm it to be true which will reinforce its message.

It has often felt like I was walking in the dark when entering a new chapter of my life. I had to take risks which could have resulted in me falling flat on my face and feeling humiliated. If it was not for my own (albeit sometimes wavering) self-confidence, then there is every chance I would have never moved forward at all.

But this is my story, and I hope that this book will provide you with all the motivation, knowledge and assurance's you require for taking control of your life, career and your long-term financial security.

While I find it awkward to talk about myself, I cannot in good conscience expect you to take my advice without telling you a little about my story so...

My name is Terence Slattery, and I was born in the United Kingdom into a working-class home in the city of Newcastle upon Tyne. I am the Director of a property investment company which I run with my fiancé Claire and I am also the Director of two other companies that specialise in business consultancy services.

It is funny as we never had much as a family when I was growing up and I was on the lower end of the social scale in comparison with the wealth of the families of my classmates in school, but around the time that I turned 8 years old, my Dad landed an impressive job.

Prior to that, my Dad had run a business fixing televisions, however, the business ended up in debt and needed to close and while my Mam had worked in a bank; she left her job when she became pregnant so for a time we had no income other than the state benefits.

My Dad being an engineer that would spend his spare time fixing televisions and other electricals meant he always had an eye for good technology. So, once he landed this new job, and we started having more money, he then started buying some remarkable gadgets for our home.

He set up a home cinema system with surround sound and a CD player. Back then the most common medium for listening to music was still via cassette tape and CD players were just starting to catch on, so it was quite the upgrade from a few years earlier.

One day though during this period of lavish tech spending my Dad came home with the ultimate cool gadget, it was a Personal Computer, simply referred to as a PC. This was the one item every kid wanted to own.

You had computers back then, but these were the ZX Spectrum, Commodore 64, Amstrad and the Amiga. The Amiga was the best of that bunch and not to turn your nose up at, but it was not a proper PC and everyone who owned an Amiga knew it and they wanted a PC.

However, as luck would have it, one day I ended up being the only kid to go into school with a PC at home. It bewildered my classmates how the poor kid had a computer better than all the wealthy kids, but life was improving for us back then.

The computer was awful by the standards of today and no kid of today's era would get their knickers in a twist about not owning one, but back in the early 1990s, it was the one thing that every kid dreamt about.

There was no internet as that craze was still to take off. It was even before the release of Windows '95 so the computer ran Microsoft Windows 3.1 as its operating system, which is so old now that you may need Google to get an idea of what it looked like.

But despite however poor it would be by today's technology standards, I loved it and it opened up my mind in a way which no teacher ever could in school.

I recall we upgraded the PC for a better version two years later with a CD Rom Drive. The first PC only had a floppy disk drive for these little blue 3.5" plastic disks, which was the technology used at the time for running all the software.

By the time we upgraded to the next model two years later, I would obsess over it. The new machine was a considerable improvement over the first, and the games were like nothing I had ever seen.

I recall my parents taking me to the computer store one day and buying me FIFA International Soccer, and that was just on another level to any football game I had ever played before.

My Dad was always tough on me with my education though, he would fly off the handle when I could not answer maths and physics questions that he would ask me and if I got no homework from school, he would set me some himself. I remember one summer he assigned me a physics project, but I just wanted to be out playing football.

He would get frustrated if I could not understand what he was explaining and then he would start shouting so to help in my development he purchased a PC programme called Microsoft Encarta.

Encarta was an interactive encyclopaedia which drew me in from the moment I first used it.

I felt I could learn anything, I just had to click into an article and read about it and then move onto the next article.

With school, the conventional classroom environment for learning did not suit me and my mind would drift. I could not focus for any prolonged period on what I found to be the most boring people talking about the most boring things, so it would not take long before I would act up and get myself into trouble.

I was a mischievous little kid who could not sit still or keep quiet, so as I transitioned from primary school to secondary school, I got lumped into a class for the more challenging students.

My classmates were not stupid, they were just more the sort who were less likely to do their homework or take interest in class, but they also were not the intellectual types neither.

When we moved into secondary school, we all got put into our classes on the first day we arrived. My cousin John who I spent most of my time with had gone to the same school a year prior to me and they had placed him into the top class. Without ever really giving it much thought, I assumed they would have also placed me into the same top class as John.

There was not an exam to determine which class we got placed into neither, nobody in primary school ever sat us down and said "now take this exam to determine which class you will get placed into when you arrive in secondary school", we just turned up on the day and found out what they had already decided.

Finding out what class they place you into was a big deal as I would have to tell my family that night and they had already expressed their intrigue to find out so there was a sense of pressure. When I was told of my class, my stomach turned. I could not believe it. I remember getting angry and saying this is bollocks, we have not even had a test, who decided this nonsense?

There were seven classes in total with each class having around thirty kids and while I knew I was not the ideal student, I felt like they would place me in one of the middle classes at the very least, the school however, had other ideas. They put me in the bottom class. Well there was one other class below me, however that only had around ten kids in it that needed more focussed teachings. Out of all the regular classes, I was at the bottom.

I am not sure how the best way to put this as I find people who brag about how smart they are and drop that they are in the likes of Mensa at every opportunity to be insufferable. I know that I am not some genius, however I do have a measurable level of intelligence which puts me in a percentile of the population which is not reflective of the class they had dropped me into at that school.

They had shafted me and this turned me off school even more. Being placed in that class meant in taking exams at 16 to determine your entire future I could not pass a single exam.

It did not matter if I provided the correct answer for every single question as the exam papers were foundation level with a capped grade. The capped grade was below the grade that merits as a pass. If you wanted to take further education you needed to pass at least four exams, however this limitation meant I could not pass a single exam I would take.

During the final two years of secondary school, my Mam tried to take me out of the school so I would not have this restriction on the exams that I would sit but it was without success as all the other local schools were full so as a result at age 16 I left school without a single qualification.

My future looked bleak at best.

My Mam, however, remained positive. It was only a few days after I finished school and she had been out shopping. She came home excited to tell me she found the local college have a service where you can retake two of your exams in case you failed them the first time around. They had limited it to only the Mathematics and English papers, however.

I thought it would make no difference as you need at least four passes if you want to take further education, but I enrolled anyway as I could see my Mam was excited.

There was no grade cap for these papers, so they included questions on topics my school teachers had never covered. I still passed both exams however.

I always resented the school for how they would treat me when I was there. The politest way I can explain it was that I had a very complex relationship with the head master. He did all he could to hold me back and make my life difficult when I would attend.

The resentment I felt however was primarily because of them

not allowing me take any worthwhile exam papers as this left me needing to make my way in life from the very bottom. Despite everything, however, I still believed in myself.

I no longer hold any resentment toward the school or the head master who made my life a misery while I was there. By needing to leave school at sixteen with no qualifications, I knew that I would need to work harder than everyone else.

I had to assume that anyone I would compete with at work would not have suffered from such poor schooling standards and they would have gone onto higher levels of education than I ever could.

This created a work ethic in me that has served me well during my career.

My Dad has provided me with invaluable wisdom and insight during my life. One of those occasions I recall visiting him at work. He had an office not like any other office I had seen, which he called his workshop.

It had a desk and a computer like a regular office, but all this other cool shit as well. There was a regular office next door with people in suits working on computers at desks, but in his workshop, it was much different. His mates would call in to visit him and talk about the football and arrange going for beers.

He had even rigged up a surround sound system in his office to play all his Rolling Stones and Pink Floyd records. I would often pop in to see him on my lunch break as both our offices were nearby one another in the city centre.

I remember joking with him one day, "how can you get away with all this setup at work?", I asked.

"I can do whatever I want son, because I always add value," he responded.

He continued, "you need to have skills that others do not and you need to do more work than others are prepared to do. Whoever you ever work for, you need to make yourself indispensable to them. Do that and nobody will give a fuck about how you go about your business".

His words combined with the fact I already knew that I would need to work harder due to my lack of school accreditations resulted in creating a mindset where I would always try to do my absolute best for whoever I was working for.

I have called the book the Value of Virtue for this reason. If we are virtuous towards the people we meet in life and the companies we work for, we will always be of great value to our society.

So, while I passed those two exam papers it was not enough to gain any meaningful further accreditations, so I did what I had to do and I made my way out into the world looking for employment.

I had to take on jobs doing the most rudimentary tasks for the lowest amount of money and slog my way up the ladder. Despite not enjoying school, I do love education and I always challenge myself to learn new skills.

As a sixteen-year-old school leaver, however, I was inexperienced and unskilled. When leaving school at that age, you primarily had two options when looking for work. There was the manual worker who would gain a trade as an apprentice or there was the unskilled office worker.

I took the path of the office worker and I would work for various organisations doing basic admin and run around tasks for short term periods. I would always get the job after the job interviews that I attended when I took on these short-term roles, so my only experience of job interviews was that I was a natural at them.

In a crushing realisation, I would later discover that this was not the case. I was working for an energy provider at this point when I applied for a promotion and encountered a real interview for the first time. Any ideas I previously held about being a natural were soon to disappear after that experience.

It was around that time however when I would become more serious about my career. I would see managers and senior managers being paid way more than I was, but yet they would start and finish work at the same times as I would. I recall thinking if I am putting in the same number of hours then it would make sense to get their job so I can get paid as much as they do.

The first internal promotion I applied for I was not even asked for an interview, which was not a great boost to my optimism.

When I enquired why they did not select me for an interview, I was told that there was a spelling mistake on my application letter so they had rejected my application.

That cannot be correct, I questioned?

When I dug deeper, I found the decision maker who reviewed the application did not know how to spell the word in question, so they dismissed my application thinking my correct spelling was incorrect.

This was frustrating, but the irony that they would not consider me for the position because of my illiteracy as determined by someone who could not spell also amused me very much.

Thankfully, I did not have long to wait after that initial rejection until I got my big break and got invited to my first interview for a promotion. This was the interview that would provide me with the reality check that I was not a 'natural' with job interviews.

I will explain more on this in the chapter about nailing the job interview, but for now, I will just say I did not land the job and my ego took quite a bruising as I came across like a mumbling idiot.

These things can make or break you though and I decided that night I would not allow it to break me and I would do every-thing I could to ensure that whenever I went for another job interview, I would never suffer from that kind of humiliation again.

This is the point that my career changed. The next interview I attended, I landed the job and got the promotion. I would con-tinue to experience this success time and time again, landing promotion after promotion.

My reputation was rising at an unprecedented rate. I became a senior employee at that company in a relatively short space of time.

Later, I would also manoeuvre myself into a role where I would work with IT on the delivery of software projects. This was an intentional move that I planned as I was interested in the work, but also, I understood that this was the area with the greatest potential earning income.

Over time, I gained enough experience working on IT projects that I could become a professional IT consultant where I could charge clients a premium rate for my services and it has been that way for almost a decade.

The key to building a successful business or career for yourself is to ensure that you always add value to your customers or company.

If you take on this mindset and follow the guidelines I will provide in this book, everything will fall into place, regardless of where you are starting from.

SCIENCE & PHILISOPHY LESSONS FOR THE COMPULSIVE SPENDER

Chapter 2

I f you have a problem with not being able to save money, I expect that you are well aware that you are not alone.

What you may not know however is just why so many of us find it difficult to save and what we can do to change that.

For many, the financial burdens of life in this day and age can be overwhelming.

In recent years salaries have not kept up with inflation, and that has made a noticeable difference to the cost of living for many people.

We have all heard of putting money aside for a rainy day, but this is difficult when you only just have enough to get by on.

Even for those who can save a little money each month, the typical saving cycle lasts only a few months until they decide to "treat themselves" and then they are right back to square one.

This repeated failure of not being able to save money is discouraging, and it turns many of us away from even attempting to save for that rainy day when we will need it most.

The thought of being frugal and going without the luxuries you have become accustomed to is also not something that one would get excited at.

"Why should I put myself through that abject misery again only to spend it all later anyway," you might ask yourself?

"You cannot spend it when you are dead" is another common justification which you might use when trying to convince yourself that spending all your income is your optimal play.

For many in our society they would consider personal finance as a crass topic which they do not feel comfortable talking about. The school system does not educate young adults on the subject of money neither, so there is no open forum for young people to learn about and discuss the subject of money.

It is my belief that this lack of discussion and education on financial management plays an important factor in why many people are struggling with their finances.

As I have already mentioned I am not the biggest supporter of the school system, but my personal bias aside I find it astonishing that there is nothing to teach children about personal finance in the secondary school curriculum.

Like it or not, money is a critical part of how our society functions and without it, your life will be a lot more challenging than it would be if you have plenty.

One thing you will see with regular occurrence are individuals that earn lots of money but still end up being broke regardless of how much they earn. I read the story of a lottery winner who won £9.7m and then blew it all on useless items and he is now back working full time for the minimum wage.

I also recall the local newspaper printing a story that stated the centre forward for Newcastle United was having money problems. He was getting bank charges for going overdrawn, but yet he was being paid £50,000 per week.

This is something I could relate with; however, I was only being paid around £12,000 per year when I was getting those charges. I estimated that he should have been receiving over £3,000,000 per year with his additional sponsorship deals.

How is it even possible he is getting bank charges for going overdrawn, I thought?

I would question if some people could ever take control of their financial situation when I have read stories such as that.

Why are some people far more compulsive than others with spending, I questioned?

I also wondered if you could provide everyone living in poverty with a large cash windfall, what percentage would end up right back in poverty like that lottery winner?

I suspect it would be a substantial volume as financial management is a learned skill that requires practice. You need to programme your mind to get excited about saving money and to dread the thought of wasting money. Without this mindset, you will continue to spend your money rather than to save and invest it.

Many view Socrates as the founding figure of Western philosophy, and he is perhaps best known for his questioning style of teaching. Plato his most well-known student would explain how Socrates would question anyone and everything.

He was a well-loved figure, but following a period of war and political turmoil resulting in the decline of Athens, those who did not share his intellect or vision targeted him as a scapegoat for the failure.

The crime that they would charge him with was the alleged corruption of the Athens youth and a failure to honour the Athenian gods.

They would give Socrates an ultimatum to renounce his philosophy or face death, but the resolve of his beliefs was unwavering as facing the court he responded, "the unexamined life is not worth living" before drinking the poison that would end his life.

His method of philosophy now referred to as Socratic questioning involves asking a clarifying question after each question until arriving at the logical conclusion.

This logical approach to internal or external thought experiments and debates is one I hold in high regard.

There have been several times during my life when I felt my mind would explode upon discovering something new.

However, it would not be the information alone that would act as the catalyst for this explosion of thought.

I would first contemplate the discovery by running various internal thought experiments while applying Socratic questioning. I can sense when I am onto something, but I need to follow the process through.

After I work my way through enough questions, I would feel a chain unlock and a floodgate open up as my mind would begin to pour with various thoughts and ideas.

One of my biggest interests is understanding how the human brain functions. Over the years I have read many books and watched countless hours of lectures on the subject.

In particular, the link between human behaviour and the brains neurochemistry fascinates me.

I can recall when I first noticed my interest in wanting to understand the human mind and I was very young; however, the memories of that evening are still vivid today.

It was a Saturday evening, and I was sitting at home watching the television.

This new show was about to start which had a hypnotist who would hypnotise members of the audience for entertainment. At this point in my life I had not even heard of hypnosis, but it sounded bizarre and intriguing.

Once the show started, the hypnotist invited willing members of the audience to the stage. He would have a joke around with the participants for a period, and then he would induce them into a state of heightened suggestibility.

I recall that he got this older gentleman from the audience on to the stage with him, and he put him into a hypnotic trance.

He then told the man that when he wakes up, he will believe he is a chicken. Then he snapped him out of the hypnotic trance, and sure enough he appeared to believe that he was a chicken.

He would peck at things and he was making chicken noises as he walked around the stage mimicking the movements of a chicken.

While for most people it was just some light-hearted entertainment which they would laugh along to, I remember at the time having a very different reaction to those around me.

I felt the tectonic plates of my world being ripped apart and rocked to their core. It blew my mind as I sat gaping at the television in amazement. It was as if he somehow had admin access to the panel which controlled the minds of these people.

I had one burning question that I needed to know and which would not get out of my head.

Could it even be possible to do such a thing, or were the audience participants just acting, and it was all a big con?

One of those occasions where I felt my mind would explode was upon first learning about hypnosis. I found a book that explained the methods of hypnosis and how you can apply the methods to hypnotise other people.

I got about two-thirds into the book, but at that point it required you to find a willing participant to practise the methods on that the final third of the book would explain.

When I asked family and friends, however, I could find nobody willing to be my guinea pig. "Not a fucking chance will I ever allow you to try that on me" was the standard response I would receive.

I had no interest in becoming a hypnotist anyway, so this was not too disappointing. My fascination was more in understanding how it worked, and I had already discovered more than I could have imagined about the human mind by that point.

The book explained how we have a conscious and a subconscious mind. The conscious mind contains the information which we are aware of at that moment and acts like a gatekeeper to determine what information it will filter into the subconscious mind, and what to disregard.

Our brain then stores everything we have encountered from

birth to the present moment in the subconscious mind, and this controls our emotions and behaviours.

Upon reading this, I drew parallels between the human brain and a computer. I thought of the conscious mind like cache memory used for processing the programmes we are running and the subconscious mind as the hard drive which contains all our personal files and operating system.

When the conscious mind receives new information, it can only hold around seven pieces of random information at one time. If you want to test this, try asking a friend to call out fifteen random numbers and then see how many of them you can recite back.

Psychologist George Miller published a paper on this titled, "The Magic Number Seven, Plus or Minus Two" in which he discusses the separate mechanisms in how the brain processes short term and long-term memory.

The subconscious mind on the other hand has an obscene amount of storage capacity. This is the part of our brain which contains our long-term memories.

Our brains will operate at different levels throughout the day depending upon the situation we are in, but it is when our brains are in a relaxed state that the subconscious mind is most open to receiving information.

Therefore, a hypnotherapist will always first try to get you into a relaxed frame of mind before starting any hypnosis session. This is also the reason why we are able to recite song lyrics without effort, despite never even trying to learn them.

When we are listening to music or watching a movie, for example, we will often be in a relaxed state of mind so this information will make its way into our subconscious mind without effort. If I ever need to learn something, I will always make sure I first feel relaxed before starting.

Upon relaxing a patient, the hypnotherapist can then make various statements or suggestions to the subconscious mind.

As the contents of our subconscious mind will help to determine how we feel and behave, this allows the hypnotherapists words to help us adjust our thought patterns and subsequently our behaviour.

What I found the most powerful after reading this book was the concept of it being the sum of our experiences stored in our subconscious mind that determines how we feel or respond to the things that occur in our day-to-day lives.

I knew I was onto something so I started running various thought experiments through my mind to better understand what that could mean and then it hit me.

I realised that we base the meaning we attach to something from our experience and understanding of it rather than from any true meaning. Continuing to think on that, I realised that we have the power to change how we let things affect us.

First, I would consider the subject of something trivial like the weather and how two individuals could have different feelings about it. I imagined one individual living in an environment that never encountered rain and when it would rain everyone would be out dancing in the street in celebration.

I thought of the positive feelings and emotions that person would feel anytime that it rained. In contrast, I then imagined another individual who had always lived in a place that would get too much rain and how they would feel miserable and depressed at the sight of it.

In both instances the event was the same, but how each individual felt about the event was a world apart. To stress test this thought experiment, I pushed the boundaries by thinking of more extreme examples.

I considered how in some culture's polygamy is very common and how those in polygamous marriages view it as normal, whereas for someone who has only lived in a culture of monogamy, the idea alone of their other half having sex with another person is enough to stir up some strong emotions never mind encountering it while they sit in the next room.

This had a very noticeable effect on how I would view the world. I felt my consciousness had opened up to a new level of understanding and I would never think of things in the same way again as I had until that point.

I find this subject of nature and nurture so interesting as while the subconscious mind plays such an important role in our behaviour it is not nurture alone, but nature that also plays a key role in each of our personalities, behaviours and the habits we form.

An interesting discovery in this area has found remarkable connections between experience and the genetic diversity of the brain. Studies suggest that our experiences can change the DNA sequence of the genome in our brain cells.

Until this point we always built the basis of any discussion around nature and nurture from the assumption that they were disparate to a large degree.

It is the connection between the brain's neurochemistry and our behaviours that I would like to focus on during this chapter however. That along with how our brain chemistry affects us regarding the inability to save money.

As a species we have been able to prosper to an unbelievable level. We have made advancements in technology to help shape the world to best suit our needs. It is our neocortex which has enabled us to solve complex problems and communicate with one another the way other animals cannot.

One challenge we now face however is that while the world and our lifestyles have advanced to levels that would have been incomprehensible to our ancestor's tens of thousands of years

THE VALUE OF VIRTUE

ago, our genetics and biology have remained the same.

We have learned through the process of evolution that all creatures will change over time to increase the probability of survival within their environment, and we as humans are no exception. Our species physiology is the way it is by grand design to help maximise our chances of survival in the world.

Over the years when I have discussed our brains biology, it often surprises people to learn that we all have such a heavy chemical dependence. Often, they will tell me they have heard this, but never had a true understanding of what it meant until I would explain.

From birth we all have a very heavy dependency on drugs. Our brain is like a little drug dealer that keeps us jacked up all day long.

Most of the opinions people have relating to drugs suffer from fantastic levels of misguidance, so this can be quite a learning curve for some. In the past people have said to me, "yeah, but they are not real drugs that our brains produce, are they?".

It is often a surprise to learn that the most powerful psychedelic drug in the world Dimethyltryptamine is a chemical that their own brain will produce. DMT, as it gets abbreviated to, is far more powerful than LSD, Ketamine, Peyote or Psilocybin Mushrooms. People also smoke it from a pipe. Does that count as a real drug I would ask?

I would follow up asking, "why do you think people seek support for addictions that do not involve ingesting any illegal chemical or substance such as gambling addiction, food addiction or sex addiction for example?"

This is not something that they will have considered, and I often get a response like, "they just have addictive personalities?" with a shrug of their shoulders.

I would then explain the brains biology and more specific the dopamine hormone and that is when things would make more sense and they start to look at addiction in a new light.

Another item people find surprising relates to the toxicity levels of various items we consume. Even things that are good for us will kill us if consume too much of them. Scientists will measure the toxicity of a substance using a system whereby they determine the LD50 factor.

The LD50 factor determines the median lethal dosage for 50% of the unfortunate rats they use as test subjects.

It often shocks people to discover that many of the legal substances they can buy are far more toxic than some other illegal substances they cannot. I would explain that our brains are producing chemicals that effect how we feel all throughout the day.

When we experience positive feelings, our brain will have released some combination of the dopamine, oxytocin, serotonin, and endorphin hormones. Our brain would release these chemicals to motivate us enough to do the things which we needed to survive as a species.

If we are feeling stressed and anxious about something, then our brain will have released the cortisol hormone which upon doing so will increase the glucose level in our bloodstream to make us feel more alert.

This again is an evolutionary process designed to enable the survival of the species and often referred to as the fight-or-flight mechanism.

One of the greatest things I ever discovered was in understanding why my brain would release these chemicals so I can behave in ways to always ensure my mental wellbeing.

This is another subject where I feel the school system needs to improve on and provide this information to young adults. More people than ever are struggling with mental health problems and the statistics regarding the increased volumes in cases of depression and suicide are heart breaking.

John Lennon once told the story that at a young age the teacher provided the children in his class with a homework assignment to write about what they wanted to be when they grew up.

He said the other kids would write stories about being firemen or doctors, but on his assignment, he only wrote a single word 'happy'.

Upon reviewing his homework, the teacher told Lennon that he must not have understood the assignment but then Lennon responded telling the teacher that they must not understand life.

Even at such a young age, he was a genius.

Happiness must be our number one aim in life. In the past I can recall hearing the quote, "money cannot buy you happiness" and I would think what a load of shit that is, but I never understood the true meaning behind the saying until later in life.

Perhaps you still think it is a load of old nonsense and that if you had lots of money, then your life would be complete, but do not be so sure.

If it was that simple then rich people would never commit suicide, but yet they still do as depression does not have a care in the world about how healthy your bank balance might be.

In recent years I can recall many rich and famous people who felt the need to take tragic action and end their lives. Chester Bennington, Keith Flint, Gary Speed and Robin Williams are just a few off the top of my head and none of those were short of money.

It is imperative that we keep our brain chemistry well balanced and we can do this by adjusting what we consume along with our behaviour and thought patterns. That magic quartet of dopamine, serotonin, oxytocin and endorphins must be looked after.

We need to do the things that result in all four hormones being released and not just one or two. If we do not we risk creating an imbalance and this leads to mental health problems including depression and addiction.

When I discovered that the chemistry of our brain affects our emotions and general state of mental wellbeing, it raised another burning question in my mind.

Like the dilemma of "which came first: the chicken or the egg?" I wondered that if our emotions are a by-product of our brain chemistry, is it even possible to change our emotions to become more positive if we do not have well-balanced brain chemistry?

For example, neuroscientists have been able to associate depleted levels of serotonin with feelings of low self-esteem. Therefore, if your brain has depleted levels of serotonin, is low self-esteem the cause of the depleted serotonin or is it the effect of it?

This was another one of those times when I felt something unlock in my brain as I was contemplating what does it mean to feel fulfilled in life and can we ever control it.

I discovered that our brains neurochemistry will change dependent upon how we live our lives and that it is something which we can influence and change by our thoughts and behaviours.

This cause-and-effect relationship between our thoughts and behaviours and our brain chemistry works like a loop. If our brain chemistry is imbalanced, then we will be prone to suffering from depression. We can however change our behaviour to increase the positive chemicals our brains produce, and this will make us feel better.

I will explain the reasons behind why our brain would produce these chemicals and how we can use our physiology to benefit our mental wellbeing in the modern world we share today.

If we are ever in pain, our brain will produce endorphins to limit the amount of pain we feel. Endorphins allow us to endure through extensive physical exercise such as running a marathon.

If you speak with someone who does a lot of long-distance running, they will often tell you about times they would become so exhausted that they felt like they would hit a metaphorical wall and crash to the ground. Then, however, they would get what they call runners high and they could continue for many more miles.

They will often also refer to this as getting a second wind.

Well, despite its name it has nothing to do with getting a second breath of wind in our lungs, but it is opioid cells within our brains releasing endorphins.

Endorphins make you feel great as opioids will do that. Drinking alcohol can do a lot of damage to our bodies, but one of the effects of alcohol consumption is that it will trigger your brain to release endorphins and dopamine.

People will often say if they have been drunk and fell over that at the initial point they fell that it did not hurt as they were drunk, however the next day they feel it.

When drunk they were encountering endorphins running throughout their body and the sole aim of endorphins is to mask pain so that is why it masks the pain at the time.

The reason our brain was designed to release endorphins however, is to ensure we could survive as a species tens of thousands of years ago. Back then, it was not as easy as just going to the supermarket to get our evening meal.

For those from our ancestors tribes that would hunt for food, the brains release of endorphins would keep them going over long periods where they would otherwise become exhausted.

We can utilise this information to help make us feel good by ensuring we get regular exercise. We do not even need to exercise with excessive intensity, just an hour brisk walking each morning will do wonders.

Our brain will also release endorphins when we laugh and smile. Therefore, it pays to keep a positive frame of mind and look to find amusement in life wherever we can.

Oxytocin is the chemical our brains produce when we are with the people that we love most in life. It is the drug of love. When you come down with a bout of the feelings and feel you might cry while watching a movie or when you feel inspired by some random act of kindness that is your brain releasing oxytocin into your bloodstream.

You might assume such qualities would not have been important for our ancestors survival, but oxytocin is vital and without it we would have died off a long time ago.

All the good conditions and behaviours in life like empathy and generosity are because of oxytocin. If you could not produce oxytocin, you could love nothing, not even your own children. Oxytocin allows us to work together to help one another.

I remember watching a nature documentary in which upon minutes of an animal being born it could already defend itself as it was being preyed upon from a predator. It had evolved in such a way that from birth it was able to defend itself by instinctively knowing to run and hide.

As humans when we are born, we cannot fend for ourselves and we heavily depend on our parents to help us survive. As we move through the circle of life and we become adults, our parents will then depend on our help.

This is still a critical part of human life today, but can you try to imagine how much more we would have relied on others in order to survive tens of thousands of years ago in the Palaeolithic era? There was certainly no home help for the elderly back in those times.

Historians have determined that we would live in small tribes and communities limited to between to 20 and 150 people.

The stronger members of the group would hunt and forage and build shelters for those more vulnerable like the elderly, and this cycle would continue with the youth, then helping the adults as they became older. Oxytocin allows us to be vulnerable and accept help from those we trust and create strong bonds with.

Having high levels of oxytocin also results in feeling more secure and assured in our lives. It boosts our immune system and increases levels of cognitive ability and problem solving.

Oxytocin also protects us against the addictive nature of dopamine.

We can all be kinder in our day-to-day life to people we come into contact with. We can try to help and encourage people rather than to judge or laugh at them if they fail.

Investing our time into relationships with friends and family does not take much. By just asking those we care about once in a while how they are feeling and what they are doing so we can see if we can support them, we will help both our own and our loved one's oxytocin levels.

Our brain produces Serotonin when we feel that we have the respect of our peers. Someone with depleted levels of serotonin will have confidence problems, whereas someone with higher levels of serotonin will feel like they can achieve anything in life.

Regardless of what anyone might say when trying to play it cool, we all love positive recognition. We like to know that we have the love and respect of our communities.

While some of us can be more self-assured and not crave recognition the way others might need it, every one of us enjoys being told when we are doing well and upon a job well done.

One beauty about Serotonin is that it is a two-way street.

When we give our support to others and they do well in something they will feel great as their brain releases serotonin, but also in return we get a hit of serotonin as we share in their accomplishment.

I will have a chapter in this book that explains how you can kill any job interview you go to. If you have struggled in job interviews, then after reading this book you then apply for a promotion and you land the job your brain will provide you with an increase of serotonin as you have increased your social status.

If you then reviewed the book thanking me for my support,

then when I read that review, I will also get a hit of serotonin.

When our social status increases, our serotonin also increases and as we give more back to society, our serotonin levels will increase again.

What I find most interesting about this is that by doing the hard things we do not necessarily want to do, but which can earn us the respect of our peers it can do more good for our mental wellbeing than just living a comfortable life where we do not push ourselves or go out of our way to help other people.

The comfortable path of least resistance can actually be the most damaging to our mental wellbeing.

I have always admired the philosophy of stoicism which encourages us to accept and embrace the hardships of life as they will help us grow during our journey through life, but I find it so fascinating that it also increases our mental wellbeing.

I imagine two teenagers living only a couple of doors apart on the same street. The street covered in a blanket of melting snow and ice from the recent bad weather they have encountered.

Both teenagers are aware that the elderly lady who lives between them will not be able to walk down the steps from her front door without slipping on the ice. The elderly neighbour will not be able to leave her house unless someone was to clear the snow and put some sand or grit down on her steps for her.

Both teenagers are sat in the comfort of their homes and are nice and warm with the fire roaring and enjoying watching the television. Neither of them wants to leave the warmth of the house to go outside to shovel snow in the freezing conditions and nobody has asked them to.

I then imagine however that they both somehow consider doing the job it at the same moment as they both know that it is a nice thing to do.

Neither of them aware of the other also considering the job, one teenager thinks about it and decides they cannot be bothered so they continue watching television and eating pizza by the warm fire.

The other teenager however despite not wanting to do it decides to go out into the cold and clear the snow and put down the grit so the elderly neighbour will not slip on the steps if she attempted to leave her house.

For that teenager, despite doing an unpleasant job out in the cold while the other teenager sat nice and comfortable watching television by doing that unpleasant job it will have done a lot more for their mental wellbeing than sitting in the warmth watching television and eating pizza did for other teenager.

By giving our life purpose and setting ambitions that we achieve, our brain will reward us with dopamine, but in addition we will also receive serotonin as we receive the respect of others due to our accomplishments and the value we add to our communities.

Dopamine is the chemical our brain rewards us with when we accomplish the tasks that we set out to achieve. It also keeps us motivated to hit our targets when we have an incentive to hit them.

It is the chemical which is most responsible for addictions and why many people struggle with compulsive spending and the inability to save money.

Say you set yourself a task list then you work your way through it all and afterwards you feel a sense of achievement and pride, well that is you high on dopamine right there.

Back as hunter-gatherers around 50,000 years ago our brains would produce dopamine to motivate our species to build shelter and hunt and forage for food, however, in today's world where we do not have such daily challenges to survive it has become very easy to hijack the dopamine neurotransmitter and release too much of the hormone without intention.

The dopamine we produce gets created in two separate parts of the brain, the first one is the substantia nigra and the dopamine from this area supports movement and speech and the second part of the brain is the ventral tegmental.

Both parts are nearby one another and the dopamine they produce relays signals that travel through the brain. While the dopamine from the substantia nigra supports movement and speech, the dopamine from the ventral tegmental is the reward drug that helps to change our behaviours and which can lead to addictions.

The ventral tegmental releases the dopamine up into our brain whenever we encounter something we like.

It is basically saying to our brain, "hey, whatever the hell that was that we just experienced, make a note of that as it is worth getting more of again".

Our brain can then motivate us to repeat certain behaviours which can then lead to the habits that we form. This can be beneficial if whatever it was that we just experienced is not detrimental to our wellbeing, but it can be dangerous if we are not careful of what we are experiencing.

To give you an example of this try to think of a time you heard a song which blew you away and then you felt the urge to discover more songs by that artist. That right there was the dopamine at work changing your behaviour to seek more of the same after you heard that first great song.

The habits we form are stored in a part of our brain which is called the basal ganglia. What is more remarkable about this is that the basal ganglia is a separate part of our brain from where we store all our memories.

There is a fascinating case study in the book 'The Power of

Habit' by Charles Duhigg in which an elderly gentleman called Eugene Pauly would change everything that science understood until that point about habits.

Eugene suffered a virus which made its way into his brain and ate its way through his brain tissue where we store all our memories.

He lost all his memories and he could not form any new memories. Remarkably however, once he had recovered from the virus and he was released from hospital to go back home after a few weeks his wife noticed that he had started to do things like go to the toilet or go for a walk and find his way back.

If you asked Eugene to tell you where he lived when he was stood outside his house he could not answer which house he lived at, nor could he tell you where his toilet was when he was sat in his living room.

However, the routine of getting up and going to the toilet or for a walk created a habit loop which would be stored in his Basal Ganglia and thus if he needed the toilet while he was sat at home then on autopilot he would just get up out of his seat and go to the toilet despite not being able to say where the toilet was located if you asked him.

By understanding how our brains function, it is a lot easier to make sense of why we can struggle to save money and why even those who earn astronomical amounts of money can still find themselves with nothing in the bank.

In most cases by the time we reach adulthood our brains are already hard-wired to want to spend money rather than to save it so just like the lottery winner who blew £9.7m or the Newcastle United striker going overdrawn on fifty grand a week unless we understand this it will not matter how much more money we earn as we will still finish up with a large waistline and a slim bank account as the saying goes.

You might question why you would be hard-wired to spend rather than save money. This is because a lifetime of programming in which spending money has resulted in you being rewarded with dopamine whereas saving money does not do that.

It would have most likely started off as a child when your parents gave you a small amount of money to go to the shop and buy some sweets with.

Right there at that moment, you will have started the programming in your mind which associated spending money with receiving a reward.

Also, there are not many catalysts for releasing dopamine like the sudden intake of high amounts of sugary treats.

As you became older and got your first pay cheque, if you purchased new designer clothes and then looked in the mirror and felt great, this is more reinforcement that is associating spending money with good feelings.

To undo all this programming, we need to enforce the message to ourselves that we are looking forward to saving money and how we want to feel excitement at seeing ourselves saving more and more money each month.

Investing the money which we save into money generating assets is the key to long term financial success, and this is something which I will cover in a later chapter, however we cannot gain money to invest without first being able to save what we earn.

The biggest challenge we face is that without the mindset that we want to save and a strong enough reason why we want to save money there is no continuous release of dopamine as a reward for saving money.

Each time we purchase something we love however like when we order our favourite take away on a weekend our brain will release dopamine.

We need to tell our brain that we want to feel excitement towards saving money and set ourselves targets and goals for the amounts we want to have saved by certain dates.

If we have a strong reason why we want to achieve this then we can also achieve the dopamine reward as our brain will reward us with dopamine whenever we achieve the targets we set out for ourselves and as an incentive to keep us motivated while in the process.

In the following chapter I will explain more on how we achieve this by ensuring that when we set goals, we specify why we are setting them.

In knowing why we want to achieve something, this will ensure our brain keeps us motivated to achieve it by releasing dopamine as we work towards realising our dreams and aspirations.

THE OBJECTIVE TREE

Chapter 3

U nless you know what your goals are, how are you ever
going to achieve them?

Goal setting is an art that will ensure we do what we need to
craft a successful life for ourselves.

It is unfortunate that it has also become one subject that many
gobshite self-help gurus have exploited with misinformation
that exaggerate the benefits.

Despite this, however, we should not underestimate the power
of setting targets and goals.

It was about a decade ago now when I was first introduced to
the Colour Code Personality Profile developed by Doctor Taylor
Hartman.

I was working at an organisation and they invited the most senior employees to a remote hotel for a development day.

During the day we all got asked to complete a set of questions
with multiple choice answers, and then at the end they would
assess our answers to determine which colours aligned with our
personality.

The room was then split into four groups with each group the
colour you were most aligned to.

It was fascinating to see how from such a simple test that

they could determine the personalities of everyone. The results were accurate beyond question, and nobody had a challenge with the group they matched to.

Those with red as the strongest colour would be decisive and pragmatic and would make great project managers. They would not have high levels of emotion in relation to a product or project, but they would ensure it would get delivered.

Yellows would have more enthusiasm about a product and would be more likely to be perfectionists. This personality profile could conflict with a strong red personality. The yellow personality would want everything to be perfect, which could risk the project not being delivered on time.

The red personality however would just care about delivering what they need to and would not care if it is not perfect the way the yellow personality would.

Blues are strong analysts and they will get into the detail before deciding on a strategy and a white personality would be philosophical and be a good visual thinker that can identify risks and opportunities others could not see.

One of my favourite writers is George Bernard Shaw, and he once stated, "You see things; and you say 'Why?' But I dream things that never were; and I say 'Why not?'".

An individual with a strong white personality profile can think like this whereas someone with a strong red personality would not comprehend saying such a thing.

Each of the personality profiles have their strengths, but also their weaknesses. In employment when finding people to work with you I believe that understanding the personality profile of an individual is a very good tool in helping you assess their suitability for the position.

I would often say to Claire that when building our business, we need to consider this in our recruitment. The best people you can hope to work with are those who have passion and virtues as they will truly care about the quality of the work they deliver and the people they are delivering it for.

If you can find those people you will have a great team, but even better again, if you can find those people but who in addition are curious and inquisitive about how things operate, then you have struck the jackpot.

Find those people and match their personality profile to the role you are looking to fill and you will build an unstoppable organisation.

With recruitment, I have always felt that the business world is behind the curve on this front. I have often lambasted that the insight you can gain from the traditional job interview alone is not enough to identify the best people to build a great business.

I remember laughing in the car with Claire at listening to the audiobook version of Principles by Ray Dalio.

When hearing his methods of recruitment, it sounded like the narrator was reading a quote of something I had said myself.

At last, somebody else is thinking this way, I exclaimed!

The reason I talk about personality profiles in this chapter is because dependent upon the personality profile you have the level at which you set your goals can differ substantially.

I created a system for my goal setting that works best for me.

Until now I have never shared this system with anyone, so I can make no claims about how effective you may find it should you use it, I just know that it is extremely effective for me.

I designed it the way I have based on my understanding of human psychology and how different personality profiles impact the level of granularity in which one thinks.

Most important, however, is that it works for me so that is why I use it.

I call it The Objective Tree.

It compromises of four components, Objectives, Goals, Tasks and Why.

I start with my objective.

This is the highest level of the components. When I know what my objective is, then I state why I want to achieve the objective.

This is the key to ensuring that I will feel adequate motivation to achieve my objective.

If we cannot list any good reasons why we want to achieve our objective then we should think of a different objective as we will not feel motivated to achieve it. We must also have an uninspiring objective for a starting point if we are unable to say why we want to achieve it so best to get it ditched.

To give you an example of an objective, you may set something like, "to equal your current salary with a secondary passive income stream from assets".

We would then list the reasons we want to achieve this objective. This may look something like the following:

Objective: Equal salary income from asset income

Why: I can retire early from employment and spend more time with my children or looking after my elderly parents who are sick

Why: I can afford to do more things I love such as travelling to exotic places I want to see which I cannot afford

Why: I can volunteer to help those suffering from an illness I feel passionately about while still being able to keep a roof over my head

Why: I can go to college and study about [insert subject] which I find really interesting

If there is something that we feel passionate about wanting when listing our 'why' this will strengthen the motivation we feel to achieve our objective.

The next component is to then list the goals we want or need to achieve to realise our objective. Our goals are at a lower level of granularity than our objective and they must relate to it.

The goals will have more focus on how we will achieve our objective so you can take action against them.

The reason I use this method where I first set an objective and then the underlying goals is that it helps me find the right level of detail. People that just set goals without doing this will often create goals that are too vague.

Our goals should be specific and measurable. Do not set a goal like, "I want to do well at work" or "I want to be rich".

This is far too vague.

Make sure our goals always relate to our objective and make sure they are specific enough that we can measure them. Using the example above we could set goals such as:

Goal: Purchase my first buy to let property

Goal: Invest £200 a month from salary into low risk investment bonds

Goal: Invest £50 a month in more high-risk company start up stocks

The final component is to then list out the tasks I am required to complete to achieve my goals.

I do this for each of my goals.

Of all the components of 'The Objective Tree' these are at the lowest level of granularity. My tasks then migrate into my 'To Do' list which I steadily work my way through.

In the above example, my first goal was to purchase a buy to let property. The tasks for that goal might look like the below:

Task: Find a mortgage broker that specialises in BTL

Task: Perform some analysis on market demand and rental rates

Task: Look for properties online in my area of choice and see if I can find any properties that I want to view

Task: Make enquiries with agents to view properties

I find using this system beneficial as it ensures that if you have a personality profile which only thinks of the bigger picture you will unearth details you had not even considered when you break your objective down into goals and tasks. It also helps those who are more task orientated to build up from their goals to create bigger picture objectives.

I am one of the world's leading experts at becoming distracted.

I find it effortless to start reading something of little value and get completely immersed into it and then wonder what the fuck have I been doing for the last hour?

Therefore, I will take any help I can get for maintaining my focus so I created this system for myself and it is the best tool I have.

I create my objective trees on the computer then print them out and stick them onto noticeboard in my office.

My 'To Do' list which includes my tasks is also kept on my mobile phone and I have it displayed as a widget on the home screen so I have a constant reminder of the workflow required to realise my goals.

This process of setting and reviewing of my personal goals provides me with great benefit as it allows me to assess the progress I am making in my life and it keeps me motivated to keep pushing myself. Life is short so we should not waste it doing tasks that do not help us achieve our objectives in life unless we are enjoying downtime.

I have often heard the advice that in working we should do what we enjoy doing. This is great advice if we can monetise what we enjoy to a sufficient enough level that we can live, however, the reality is for most people they go to work to get the income required to keep a roof over their heads and put food on the table.

Even if we enjoy going to work each day as we get on well with our colleagues, the chances are if money was not a factor in our life as we had won the national lottery then we could no doubt find far more enjoyable and rewarding ways to fill out our days other than going into the office and chatting to Susan about last night's Coronation Street.

I have heard stories of people who have won the national lottery and then returned to work as it would bore them just sitting around the house with nothing to do after leaving their employer.

For adults, I find Boredom to be a ridiculous concept in all honesty. I once read a quote that stated something like "boredom is the desire for desires" which sums it up just nicely.

Can we not think of anything which we would enjoy doing if we did not need to go to work to get the money needed to survive?

We could do a lot of travelling, play video games, volunteer to help people in need or give ourselves creative projects to work on that we could get invested into such as writing books, creating TV shows or writing and recording songs.

There are many courses we could take to learn more about the subjects we find interesting.

The truth is, we all go to work for money; therefore it makes sense to think ahead about how we can ensure that we can bring home as much money from the time that we spend working.

I recall when starting out in my career and when working in various offices that some employees would wear an identification badge that differed from everybody else's badges. For example, the ribbon which would go around their neck would be a different colour to everybody else.

Being the curious type, I wondered why this was so I asked, "why is it we have a blue ribbon and others have a red ribbon on their passes?"

Those wearing red ribbons are IT contractors. Specialist resource that they pay a fortune for that work on IT projects. This was as much as I was told however.

Not content to leave it at that however, I would continue to research this strange phenomenon of IT contractors.

How much do they earn?

What is it they do?

How did they become what they are?

All these questions were flowing through me as I delved into understanding more about them.

After completing my analysis, I determined that this was the career route that I wanted to take.

This is the career that will be my best option to maximise my earnings while in employment, I thought.

I found out that there were many various roles and career paths that one could take to become an IT contractor, for example, there is the role of the Programme Manager, Project Manager, Business Analyst, Developer, Solution Architect and Tester to name some of the most common roles.

The key thing which linked these roles is that they all played a part in delivering change projects to the IT landscape of a business or organisation.

The path to becoming an IT contractor requires you to first work as a permanent employee on various change projects as a junior member of the change team that is still learning the ropes of their trade.

Then when you have a sufficient enough level of experience and expertise you can then transition to become an IT contractor.

Companies assign projects with capital expenditure funding to deliver the project to the company that the contractors are working for.

The company will grant funding for a project based on the benefits of delivering the project. So, in a typical example, if a project will provide a net benefit of £5M, but it has a cost to deliver the project of £700k then it does not matter that the company is spending £700k as without spending that money they would not realise the £5M benefit.

It also includes the cost of the contractors to work on the project within the £700k cost to deliver it.

While the company could reduce the overall cost to deliver the project by appointing cheaper junior change professionals this could put the project at risk of not realising the £5M benefit case.

Therefore, you must not even consider becoming a contractor unless you are an experienced change professional that will not derail a project by making mistakes that an experienced change professional would not.

To put it another way, if you want the big money, you must first earn your stripes.

I knew that if I wanted to earn big money as an IT Contractor I needed to first find a way of getting sufficient enough experience as a junior change professional.

Using my objective tree, I put into place a roadmap of goals that would allow me to realise my objective.

I had already encountered success in my previous interview and I was now working as a supervisor so the next logical progression for someone in my position was to apply for the role of a manager.

I knew when looking at that career progression path however that if I took that path and then I was to gain promotion again that I would find myself in middle management at the level of regional manager / service manager / operational manager.

Good positions that paid well enough and had a lot of prestige as a permanent employee in an organisation, but those positions would not allow me to become an IT consultant where I could receive three times their income.

There was an intranet site at the company I was working in which they would post job openings for employees to apply for and there was a position which opened up for a junior change analyst.

The grade of the position was the same level I was already at so it seemed strange for someone in my position to apply for it as it would have been a side step to move into a new department with less prestige than someone who is a manager of people.

I knew however that I had to make that sidestep to get the experience I would require to become a senior change professional that could transition into the role of an IT contractor so without hesitation I uploaded my CV and covering letter and I applied for the position.

They invited me to the interview and then not too long afterward they offered me the job. Now I could embark on my new career path of learning the ropes as a junior IT professional.

I would report into a Development Manager and I worked on projects providing analysis and testing and when I had sufficient experience I could then apply for another promotion.

Over the next number of years, I kept encountering success when applying for various change management positions each time taking on new roles and expanding my knowledge and experience of working on IT projects.

I became a Continuous Improvement Manager where I discovered all about lean principles and six sigma techniques which is invaluable business knowledge that I recommend for everyone.

Then I would also work as a Development Manager across various change projects before taking on the role of a Test Assurance Manager on a large £200M software migration project.

I kept working hard and growing in my knowledge and experience until the point when I knew I could transition to an IT contractor.

It was not by luck that I found myself in the positions I did, it was after putting into place a well thought out plan in which I knew that if I followed that plan it would lead me to where I needed to get to.

This meant taking what appeared to be a side step during my career, but that one sidestep that I took was the biggest leap forward I ever made in the overall progression of my career.

If I never knew what my objectives were then I would not have even considered taking that side step.

For some personalities they can see the big picture and they know what they want in life, however for many it is not so easy therefore setting goals and objectives can be extremely beneficial.

I have said it before but I will say it again, you need to know what your goals are if you are to ever have any chance of achieving them.

NAILING THE JOB INTERVIEW

Chapter 4

R egardless of the outcome, I have a lot of respect for anyone that applies for a promotion within the company that they are working.

Your brain is your greatest asset, however that same brain of yours can also be an unsupportive arsehole when you need it most.

It takes a certain amount of courage to even apply for an internal promotion.

Often it is not even the fear of the interview or failure to land the job that holds many back, but just the mere thought of the application process alone can be daunting.

How will my colleagues feel about it, you might question?

I have only worked here for a short period and there are people who have worked here for a decade, would they even respect me as their superior?

What if the role is too challenging or I dislike it, I enjoy my current job?

These are the thoughts and self-doubts that we all encounter at some stage during our careers.

The successful people who have gained promotion into senior positions at your company are not immune to nerves and fear, they have just learned to overcome them.

The biggest obstacle that many of us face is to overcome those nerves and fears so we can put ourselves into positions where we can fail.

Those same daunting positions where we can fail are also the positions we need to be in to win. Staying where you are and doing what you already do is easy, but that is not how you win at life.

There is a great scene between the boxer Rocky and his son from the movie Rocky Balboa.

His son, bemoaning being the son of his famous Dad is feeling sorry for himself and blaming his Dad for how his life is going.

Rocky having none of it responds to his son telling him, *"Life ain't about how hard you hit. It's about how hard you can get hit and keep moving forward. That's how winning is done! Now if you know what you're worth, then go out and get what you're worth, but you gotta be willing to take the hits, and not pointing fingers saying you ain't where you wanna be because of him, or her, or anybody. Cowards do that and that ain't you. You're better than that!"*

That mindset of taking personal ownership and accountability for your life is something I have great respect for.

If your life is not how you want it to be then do not blame other people, but take action to change it. We can all encounter times we feel sorry for ourselves, but there are many humbling stories from people that have suffered far greater hardships and have not let it hold them back.

This is the winning mindset we need in order to overcome that first obstacle to apply for the promotion and it takes courage. It is back to that stoic philosophy of embracing struggle by stepping out of our comfort zone helps us to grow and develop, but in addition to get the most out of life.

I can remember the first time I attended a job interview that was not for an entry-level job. It is not a fond memory as I remember being ripped apart during the interview and it was not a pleasant experience.

I was young and I turned up for the interview looking sharp and thinking it will be a formality as I had always encountered success in my previous job interviews when going for an entry-level positions.

I therefore made the mistake of assuming that I was a natural, but I was in for a big shock.

It was the first time I had encountered a competency-based interview. A competency-based interview means they ask you questions where you need to provide specific examples of times when you have carried out certain tasks which in doing so shows a level of competence in a particular area.

They do not specify what competency the interviewer is looking for and the interview question can mask it, however it can be easy enough to determine some practice.

These interviews are easy when you know what you are doing, but as a young eager buck who had never experienced one before it did not take long before it got awkward in there.

I remember trying to control my sweaty hands from shaking as my dried-out mouth made lots of noises without ever saying anything.

Unimpressed by my answers, the stern woman who was interviewing me kept applying more pressure by asking for better answers each time I answered.

This is horrific, what on earth was I thinking? I just wanted it to be over.

I came across terrible and I made a total arse of myself.

You know that feeling of relief when you need the toilet and it is touch and go if you will make it in time or not and you reach the toilet just in the nick of time, well that is nothing compared to the relief I felt when the interview ended and I was able to leave the room.

I knew I would not get the job so I did not care about hearing the formal result to see who they would appoint as there was no way that it could have been me, I thought.

The only thing that could have gone in my favour is that all of the other interview candidates I spoke to said they also suffered the same fate and some even vowed to never apply for another promotion again.

Even still, I knew it could not have been me that they would have wanted for the job after that interview.

That evening though I went home and I vowed to never allow that to happen again. I needed to learn how to handle myself in job interviews and become good at them.

After searching online, I found quite a hefty book on the subject so I downloaded it and read it cover to cover.

I also made a note on my computer of all the questions that I could remember being asked during the interview and this was the start of what resulted in me going from getting crucified in that job interview to smashing all of my next ones.

I kept this file which held the questions they had asked me in the interview on my computer and I would append it with new questions each time I went for another job interview.

Funnily enough, I found that the same questions would continue to come up. Sometimes the wording of the question would be different, but ultimately, they were asking the same thing.

This is something which surprised me over the years as each time I would go for new promotions I would expect the interview questions to become more challenging but I have had the same questions come up for positions that were paying £15,000 and £150,000 per year.

The most notable difference is the quality of the other candidates you are competing against will increase when you go for more senior positions.

You will also sometimes get asked to produce presentations and to take exams for the more senior roles, but the interview itself does not change much.

I have known many people worry about needing to produce presentations for job interviews but these can be even easier than the interview itself.

One of the most common mistakes people make when presenting is to produce a set of slides they fill with text and then stand in front of the audience reading from the slides that are being projected onto the wall.

If you need to produce some slides and give a ten-minute presentation on a subject it is always best to keep the slides clear with minimal text, just the bullet points of what you want to talk about.

You should learn what you want to say word for word for each slide so you do not even need to look at the slides. The slides should be for the audience and not a prop for you.

By not needing to look at the slides you can then keep your eyes on the audience which will keep them engaged with what you are saying.

I learned that to answer a competency-based question there is a technique which you should deploy which ensures you answer the question forgetting no key elements of the answer.

It also prevents you from rambling a load of nonsensical jibberish while making lots of thinking noises like "erm" followed by a few seconds of pausing and then another "erm".

I also learned that it is important to ask your own questions at the end of the interview and how to deploy certain psychology tricks that would help me come out on top.

Using my trusty document of all the questions I had ever encountered, I would bullet point each question and then underneath I would type out my perfect answer in a structured way using the technique that prevents you from forgetting any parts of the answer and from waffling on a load of shite.

I would then read the answers back until I could recite them word for word like the back of my hand.

By doing this it would compose me the next time I would then go for a job interview and I would answer whatever got sent my way in a concise manner without stuttering on and making strange thinking noises.

Once the interviewer had finished asking all their questions, I would ask questions of the interviewer, good solid questions which would put the interviewer on the back foot and I would always finish up with my trusty finishing question which allowed me to end the interview in complete control.

Time and time again, I would find out I had landed the job.

I knew I was competent enough to do the jobs I was applying for so I just needed to ensure I would not fall at the first hurdle of the interview and this method of mine allowed me to breeze through the interview process.

Once I was in the new position I would exceed expectations by giving my all to it while also gathering more experience and better examples for future interview questions until I would go for the next promotion and so the cycle would continue.

I will now explain to you how you can do the same by explaining the correct way to answer these questions and to provide you with examples of the questions I have encountered in my past interviews.

Also I will tell you some of the more left-field questions I have encountered during interviews and how I would answer those and I will also provide you with the questions I would ask of the interviewer myself at the end of the interview as well as how I would always close out the interview.

The first thing we will cover is how you should answer the interview questions by using a method called the STAR technique. STAR is an acronym for situation, task, action, and result.

If you can additionally include anything that you learned as a result of your experience then you should also include this within your response.

Another methodology other than STAR for answering interview questions is the CARL methodology. CARL requires your answers are structured with the elements of: Context, Action, Result, and Learnings.

With CARL the context is the same as the scenario from STAR, then both share the Action and Result, however you have an additional element for Learnings with CARL that you do not have with STAR.

I find however that you can have great examples to competency based questions that you do not have any learning from so I prefer to use the STAR methodology, but to include Learnings in the result element of my answer when applicable.

So, let us assume you are asked a competency-based question which might go something like: -

"Can you tell me about a time when during the last six months you have gone above and beyond to deliver a higher level of service to our business?"

Now using the star technique what you would do is answer the question by first stating what the situation or scenario was and then you would specify what task you had to complete before expanding on that with the specific actions that you had taken and you would finish up by advising what the results of your actions were.

The greater the results the better it would reflect on the example you provided for your answer.

As long as we want to do well and progress in our career we should all have many of examples where we can show particular competencies to answer these kinds of questions.

The challenge however, is in that very moment they ask you the question to flick through your memories to determine and then recite the optimal example coherently.

Therefore, I find my method of updating my interview sheet works best as you can take your time to think about the best examples you can provide without any pressure and then learn your answers by reading your interview sheet at home until it becomes second nature.

I would print my interview sheet out which had the questions and my answers underneath and then I would ask family members to interview me asking questions in a random order and they could mark me on how well I answered the question based on the answer they had in front of them and which I was reciting from my mind.

Everyone has different examples to answer competency-based questions so you need to determine your own examples and while I can tell you the questions you are likely to encounter in the interview and I cannot just give you the answers to them as my answers will be different to yours as we will have different levels of experience and will have worked in different roles.

To give you an example though, let us say you work at an entry level position in a call centre for a bank and you are going for your first promotion and you got asked the competency-based question I provided earlier about going above and beyond in your role. Using the STAR technique your answer might go something like: -

"Can you tell me about a time when during the last six months you have gone above and beyond to deliver a higher level of service to our business?"

"Sure, I was working on the phones for customer support when I received a phone call from a distressed elderly lady. She had contacted the bank to state she had sent a large transaction to a family member and the family member had not received the funds; however the money had left the elderly ladies account. She had concerns that perhaps she had sent it to the wrong account and that it could not be retrieved.

The phone call hit the switchboard at 16:57 on a Friday evening and I was to finish work in three minutes and it was also my weekend off so my partner and I had planned to go away for the weekend.

I could sense that the customer was in a state of distress so I re-assured the customer that I would resolve the problem for her. The call lasted for almost thirty minutes as I tried to resolve the issue, but unfortunately, I required someone from the transfers team to update me on the status of the transaction. Each Friday the transfers team all finish work at 16:30 however and they would not be back in the office until tomorrow morning.

This meant I had to explain to the customer that the trans-action is most likely still on its way to her relatives account, but to verify I need a transfer agent to log onto their system. I informed the customer I do not have access to that system to view where the funds are in the transfer process, but someone from the transfers team would be back in the office in the morn-ing.

Explaining to the customer that I will be back in the office on Monday, however I could have a colleague call her back the fol-lowing morning to provide her with an update, the customer asked if I could update her tomorrow instead as she did not want to speak to anyone else. I told the customer that would be fine and she thanked me.

That evening I went home and I explained to my partner we needed to cancel our weekend plans as I would have to go into the office in the morning as something had come up which they needed me for.

I went to the office on Saturday morning and got the update from the transfer team. Thankfully the payment was still in the transfer process and had not went into somebody else's bank as the customer had feared. The transfers agent advised that as the payment was for a large amount it needed a manager to authorise the transfer which is why it was taking longer to process, but that the manager was next to the agent so they would do that right away and it would then be available for the recipient in around 4 hours.

I then called the elderly lady back up and advised her of this and she was so relieved. She thanked me and then wrote a letter to my manager thanking me for my service and also sent a box of chocolates to the office for me with a thank you card which was nice."

Notice how at the start of the answer I stated what the scenario/situation was (call coming in, home time, weekend booked off, distressed customer) then I explain what my task was (resolve the customers concerns) then I stated what actions I took (calmed customer down, stayed late, cancelled weekend plans, came in on weekend off, got payment authorised, updated customer) and then I stated what the result of my actions were (happy customer, positive feedback, thank you card and chocolates).

I have never actually worked in a bank call centre so I just made that answer up on as an example of how you would answer that kind of question using the STAR method.

This is just to give you an idea of how you can answer these questions, but by using your own examples from your own experiences within your career.

I am going to now provide you with a list of competency-based interview questions so you can create your own document and then you can populate the answers for each question using your own personal examples while using the STAR technique.

Underneath each question I will put a line item for you to add key words for each part of your answer so that if you have the paperback copy of this book you can make some notes to help you in planning your full answer later when you write up your complete answers on the document you create.

I will also add an optional line for any keynotes that relate to learnings you may have obtained as a result of your experience.

Can you tell me the last time you updated your own area of expertise including the reason for the update, your methods, and the outcome?

S ....

T ....

A ....

R ....

(L) ....

Can you tell me about a time when you have had to learn a technical procedure?

S   ....

T   ....

A   ....

R   ....

(L) ....

Tell me about a time when you have shared your knowledge with others in your team or business area to improve a business process or procedure?

S   ....

T   ....

A   ....

R   ....

(L)   ....

Tell me about a time when you have had to pull together with colleagues to achieve an end goal with limited time and how you achieved the goal?

S ....

T ....

A ....

R ....

(L) ....

Can you describe a situation where you have identified a problem through analysis and what steps you took to prevent or resolve the issue?

S ....

T ....

A ....

R ....

(L) ....

Can you give me an example of a time when you have made a decision which was outside of normal procedures or business practices but which benefited the business?

S   ....

T   ....

A   ....

R   ....

(L)   ....

Tell me about a time when you have anticipated and therefore avoided a problem from arising?

S   ....

T   ....

A   ....

R   ....

(L)   ....

Give me an example of a time when you have been able to persuade someone to do something where they were opposed to it, what approach did you take and what was the outcome?

S ....

T ....

A ....

R ....

(L) ....

Tell me about a time when you have identified an expert to support you to deliver something you needed support with, how did you identify their expertise and how did you approach them for assistance?

S ....

T ....

A ....

R ....

(L) ....

Tell me about a time when you have set personal goals to achieve a work objective?

S   ....

T   ....

A   ....

R   ....

(L)   ....

Give me an example of a time when you have had to lead a team to meet targets and deadlines?

S ....

T ....

A ....

R ....

(L) ....

Can you provide me with details of a time where you have motivated individuals to achieve their objectives resulting in an increase in the work level?

S ....

T ....

A ....

R ....

(L) ....

Can you describe for me a situation where you have been under pressure to produce results?

S ....

T ....

A ....

R ....

(L) ....

Give me an example of when you have had two pieces of work to deliver at the same time within a limited timeframe, how did you manage your time and what considerations did you make to deliver the work?

S ....

T ....

A ....

R ....

(L) ....

Can you provide me with an example of a time when you have had to react to change in the work place and how you reacted and what the outcome was?

S   ....

T   ....

A   ....

R   ....

(L)   ....

Tell me about a time when you have had to provide a higher level of customer service than what is expected to either internal or external customers?

S ....

T ....

A ....

R ....

(L) ....

Describe for me a situation where you have had to deal with a customer or stakeholder who has made an unrealistic demand?

S   ....

T   ....

A   ....

R   ....

(L)   ....

Can you provide me with an example where you have taken action beyond normal expectation to add value to a customer?

S ....

T ....

A ....

R ....

(L) ....

You are also likely to get at least one or two non-competency-based questions in any interview you attend so I would also make a note of those when they came up.

These questions do not need to be answered using the STAR technique, but if you can still recite your answer word for word in your mind before you have even been asked the question then when they come up in the interview you will come out of the interview looking composed so you should also practice for these kinds of questions.

These questions are often easy enough but they can also throw you off guard if you are not prepared for them.

Some of the more left field ones you cannot anticipate and you will have to answer on the fly when you get asked one you have not been asked before, but here are some of the common non competency-based questions you may encounter when applying for positions during your career.

As with the above competency based questions, I will leave space underneath so that you can make notes for your answer if you have the paperback copy of this book.

Tell me about what your current position entails and how long you have been working in it?

....

....

....

....

What do you think the role you are applying for entails?

....

....

....

....

What are your biggest individual strengths and weaknesses?

....

....

....

....

If an incident occurred that you thought was wrong and breached company rules, how would you approach this?

....

....

....

....

Why do you think you have the skills to carry out this role?

....

....

....

....

How do you motivate yourself when there is too much or too little work?

....

....

....

....

How would you approach a colleague that had made errors in their work and how would you handle the situation if you felt that the colleague was not listening to you when you approached them about it?

....

....

....

....

How would you handle a conflict between two colleagues at work if your line manager was unavailable?

....

....

....

....

Why is work process documentation an important part of the job?

....

....

....

....

How would you deal with a colleague who also applied for this
position if they were unsuccessful and you got the job and you
felt they resented you for it?

....

....

....

....

Now here are some of the more left-field questions I have been asked during interviews.

You have no way of preparing for these if you have not ever encountered them before, so anytime they do arise make a note and add them to your document in case of the off chance you get them again and then you will be better prepared.

The interviewer may try and persuade you that these kinds of questions are unimportant and that it is just a bit of fun with no right or wrong answer, however it is always best to still answer using logic and keeping the focus of your answer business related.

Imagine I am an old aged pensioner who has very limited knowledge of computers and technology, now can you explain Twitter to me?

....

....

....

....

If you could go out for lunch and drinks to discuss any topic of your choice with anyone alive or dead who would you pick?

....

....

....

....

If I asked you to tell me exactly how many windows there are in London what would your answer be?

....

....

....

....

The next section I want to cover in this chapter relates to the questions you ask yourself at the end of the interview. This is not a polite way for the interviewer to say time is up and it is a legitimate question which you should always answer yes to.

You should be intrigued about the position you are applying for so it makes sense to have questions and it shows that you are interested.

You can ask whatever you feel is appropriate based upon the position you are applying for so there is no fixed set of questions to ask, but I will show you the kind of questions that I would ask to give you an idea.

While it is the interviewer who will need to answer these questions I will still leave space underneath each question so that you can think about how you would answer each question if they were asked of you.

By anticipating how the interviewer may respond to your questions you can think of possible follow up questions to keep the conversation flowing and ensure you get an answer with sufficient enough detail that you are wanting from the answer.

What do you think the biggest challenge will be for the successful applicant?

....

....

....

....

How do you see the role and the department expanding and integrating with other business areas over the next couple of years?

....

....

....

....

What do you think the most important skills are to ensure the successful applicant will perform well in the role?

....

....

....

....

You can always ask more questions at the end of the interview and the ones I mentioned are just an example of some of the questions I have asked myself over the years.

To finish the interview, I would perform my party trick. I would always finish up the interview with the same question.

It is a rhetorical question in which I am confident of knowing how the interviewer will respond. The question is not really even a question and is more just a way to close out the interview, but it ensures I would always end the interview strongly.

I would appear to be searching my mind for anything else I wanted to ask by moving my eyes as if I am looking at something in the top left corner of the room (which subconsciously indicates that someone is thinking) and then I would say,

"No that is everything from me unless you would like to ask me anything more to help you with my application?"

The interviewers would always reply with, "erm no I think that covers everything from us".

Then I would close out the interview by replying with "well thank you very much for your time and I will look forward to hearing from you". We would then shake hands and I would leave the interview room.

The key thing in this final transaction is that it is me rather than the interviewer who closed out the interview.

This gives off an impression of power and control and it is something most of your competition will not be doing at the end of their interviews.

When the interviewers come to scoring each candidate on how well they performed in the interview they will remember you and how you closed out the interview in control and as long as you had good answers for all the questions they asked then you will be in a very good position to land that promotion.

The key to landing the job when you have the interview is preparation. If you prepare using the guidelines above you will absolutely walk any interview you go to. You need to know your answers to all the questions like the back of your hand though.

As the saying goes, "fail to prepare and prepare to fail".

WORK ETHICS & VIRTUES

Chapter 5

P assion and virtue are the parents of hard work.

If you care about the work you do and the company or custom-ers you do it for, a natural by-product of this is that you will work hard.

Working with passion is so much more than just working hard. Someone who works hard can be a great asset, but it would be a surprise to find someone who is willing to give everything if they have no passion or virtues for the work they do or the com-pany they are doing it for.

Passion motivates and encourages us to work hard and to care about the standard and quality of the work we deliver.

Over the years I have seen many people go to work each day without ever applying themselves and just doing the minimum amount of work required to get by, and I just think why waste your time like that?

Once you have dragged yourself out of bed in the morning and made the journey into work, you have done the hardest part and now that you are there you might as well make an impact by getting your head down and getting through more work than all of your colleagues.

Trust me when I tell you that this does not go unnoticed by your line managers.

I knew I would have to work hard as I had to start at the bottom, but this is just as important for someone who has a wealth of experience and accreditations.

Let me put it this way, let us assume you are a business owner and you have a backlog of customer complaints which you need someone to work through so you go online and list the position and start taking interviews.

Upon interviewing all the candidates and then taking on the successful applicant who do you think would be more valuable to you out of someone with no qualifications nor any experience, but who got their head down and worked flat out clearing as many customer complaints as they could or someone with a degree and lots of experience but who would keep getting the coffees in and chatting about what was on TV?

The only thing which the business owner is interested in is seeing the backlog of complaints going down with high-quality work and any experience or formal accreditations mean nothing if you do not deliver the results which the business owner is looking for.

Anyone will gain sufficient experience over time and accreditations mean nothing if you do not have a strong work ethic. Finding an employee who will give them everything is what an employer wants more than anything.

That individual will get experience if they do not have much and they will be happy to pay to send them on courses, because they know that the employee will keep delivering value because they have integrity and passion for the company and the work they do.

One small item which will go a long way is to just work an extra hour more than everyone else each day. This can allow the traffic to calm down so you do not get home much later than you would have if you left at your regular time but in that extra hour if you can clear another five tasks or customer queries then at the end of the month when the line manager looks at the output of the team you will have completed around 100 more jobs than all of your colleagues.

In my last contract, I would get a sandwich from the hotel next door and bring it back to my desk where I would eat it and then work again, only ever taking around ten minutes per day for my lunch.

I was new to an industry which was very complex, so I knew I had to work hard to get myself up to speed enough so I could add value to that business.

I would also make sure I logged on when back at home on an evening and I would respond to all the emails I had received that day, which I never had time to get to during the day. Often, I would work until the early hours of the morning.

I have worked with this level of commitment as both an employee of companies and for clients I have worked with as a consultant contractor. I believe we all have a moral obligation to deliver value for whoever is paying our wages.

I believe those without this mindset will ultimately end up delivering a lower standard of work to their customers, and this will hinder them during their career.

As a self-employed consultant, you enter a contract between the client company and your own company. This is a different dynamic to working for a company as an employee, as it is a business to business (B2B) relationship.

In a B2B relationship, there is nothing to protect you as the worker providing services to the client's business the way there is if you were an employee of the client's business.

If you mess around and do not deliver results, then the client can just end your contract with immediate effect without having to worry about taking you through a lengthy process of disciplinary hearings and involving Human Resources (HR) as they would with one of their own employees.

You also charge the client a premium rate for your services that is a lot higher than the equivalent permanent employee salary for that position so again try to think about of it through the eyes of the business owner.

If it was your business, and you had someone that was invoicing you for such large amounts each month, do you think you would continue to pay them that money if they did not work hard and add value?

It is an unfortunate reality, but over the years I have seen several self-employed contractors have their contracts finish without a moment's notice from the clients we have been working at together.

The dollar signs attract people, but if you charge big money, you need to have the right mindset and understand that you need to deliver value or you will find the client will drop you like a bad habit.

As you move into more senior positions during your career, the roles which you take on will become more challenging. You will have more to learn with higher volumes of work to deliver, and you will need to deal with more senior stakeholders with bigger demands than ever before.

Therefore, you cannot ever take your foot off the gas and why even as a very experienced IT professional with a past record of always delivering results, I still work as hard today as I did when I first started out.

The moment you become complacent then your work will suffer, and a client will not tolerate it.

Also, as you progress through your career into more senior roles, they will expect you to have a sufficient level of knowledge of the business area which you are working in so you can add value.

At this level, it is no longer just a case of keeping your head down and putting in the hours; you need to be using your brain, identifying risks and opportunities and making recommendations, however, if you do not have a good enough understanding of the business area which you are working in this is something you will struggle with.

I once read a book that stated the hardest three words in the English language for anyone to come out and say are, "I don't know".

This is something I find especially true at senior levels of large corporations as there is an expectation that you know what you are doing, so nobody wants to look incompetent by saying they do not know up at that level.

I firmly believe however that we should never be afraid to say when we do not know the answer to something, but also just as firmly believe that when we identify something we do not know that we make every effort to find out the answer to it.

Only by accepting what we do not know are we able to seek information to learn.

I find someone that is prepared to state that they do not know something and ask about it far more refreshing than someone who keeps quiet, pretending that they know as they are too afraid for fear of being judged.

I can give you a good example of this actually from my last contract. I had been working in Surrey in the south of England for the UK's largest energy supplier, and I had been there for coming up to two years when my contract was approaching renewal. The parent company had also recently purchased an energy company in Ireland.

I was working from home one day when my line manager phoned me up to discuss my contract situation, he said, "Terence, I just wanted to have a quick chat about your contract, there is an opportunity to work on a project over in Ireland," he then stated, "you have worked in this sector for many years now at different organisations so I was wondering if you have had any experience of working on settlements?".

I had some experience of working on a project at an energy supplier in which we amended the way retail customers were invoiced on estimated readings to reduce a gap in settlements, so I advised him of this.

However, I also stated that other than that one project my experience of settlements is non existent so I asked him if he could tell me more about the role so I could determine if I would be suitable or not.

He told me not to worry and that I would be perfect for it, and then he asked if I would be prepared to go to Ireland for three months to work on the project. He followed up with "It is only a small bit of work, three months at most then you will return to us here in the UK".

Sure, I told him, no problem. I asked him if it was definitely only going to be for three months as if so I would keep paying for my bedsit room by the office in the UK.

"Absolutely," he told me, "three months at most, it should be a really straight forward project".

We agreed I would do the job and then I started looking for a home to rent in Ireland while getting ready to work on my new project.

We found a nice little place to rent in Kinsale so Claire and I packed all our stuff and drove from Surrey to Wales where we got the ferry and then drove down to Cork where we would stay for the next three months.

When I got to the office for my first day I had still received very little detail from anyone about what it was I was to be working on other than it was a small piece of work which would last for three months and that it related to settlements in some way.

It did not take long for me to realise that the amount of work needed would take more like three years and that I was also now working in an industry which I had zero experience or knowledge of working in.

It also turned out to be the most complex industry I am yet to work in.

Until this point all the projects which I had worked on in the energy industry were in the retail business. This new role however was for the assets and trading element of the energy industry.

Assets being the generators which produce power and trading being the hedging strategies with financial instruments like CfD's.

In the office, there were several boardrooms, and they named each of them after a famous Irish writer. For example, there was a Wilde meeting room named after Oscar Wilde, a Shaw meeting room named after George Bernard Shaw and so on.

I recall in my first week being in a meeting in the largest boardroom with approximately 17 other senior business leaders and consultants.

Everyone knew I had come from the UK, where the wholesale market had a lot of similarities with the proposed wholesale market Ireland would transition into as part of this project.

It appeared that there was some crossed wires however as they all seemed to think that I had experience in the UK wholesale market (which I did not and I knew zero about it as I had always worked in energy retail).

I recall during the meeting one consultant just switched to me out of the blue and asked me what my thoughts were on the approach they had been discussing.

I had been quietly taking notes up until this point, so the direct question came at me as quite a surprise. Everyone's eyes fixed onto me as they were all ready to hang off my every word.

The problem was, I did not have a clue. I was completely out of my depth. I was also experienced enough however that I could have bullshitted my way through a response without breaking a sweat. If I did that, however, I would not have been being true to the client, nor my own moral standards.

It would have been simple, all I would have had to respond with would have been something like, "no it all sounds good, you have the basis of it covered and a good foundation to build from and the proposed approach sounds sensible and pragmatic and what I would also recommend".

At which point the conversion would then move onto the next item with everyone reassured that everything was fine.

Instead, however, I told the truth. I responded,

"well it is fitting that these meeting rooms are named after famous Irish writers as after only a few days of being here I have filled up two large notepads from cover to cover with the notes that I have taken already as I do not have the first idea about half of the things which have been discussed so unfortunately I will need to get a better understanding of the business and the change we are delivering before I can provide any valuable input".

There was an awkward silence for a moment until one of the

more senior members of the programme made a joke about my honesty and then the meeting continued.

What is important though is after that and every other meeting I attended I was studying like crazy to get up to speed.

Those first six months I worked until around 3am every single night, and I would also work all weekend studying how that industry operated.

I would go home and read up on all the things I had taken notes on during the day. On my computer I would watch lectures on YouTube about how combined cycle gas turbine power plants would operate and I would read Investopedia for hours at a time learning about how various financial instruments like CfD's worked in trading.

Back when my Dad would assign me physics assignments, I used to think that I will never need to know about any of this stuff, but I found myself recalling lessons on the difference between energy and power for that job as well. The learning curve I was on was huge.

I would also set meetings to sit with various managers within the business to ask them questions and walk me through what they did each day.

I was transparent about my lack of knowledge in the sector, and this was liberating as it allowed me to ask all the questions I needed to help me to get up to speed without fear of being judged.

I knew I had the skills and experience from working on IT projects to know that I could do as good a job as anyone if I knew how the business operated, but I also knew that unless I had a sufficient level of knowledge in relation to how the business operated that I would not have been able to add the value required to the client.

I quote Albert Einstein as saying, "I am neither clever nor gifted. I am only passionately curious". I have often stated that to find great employees one of the best metrics you can look for is the curiosity of the individual.

Someone who is curious is open to the idea that everything they know might be incorrect, and they are also cognisant of just how little they know so they will seek information to continue in their learning and development.

The potential for this kind of individual is limitless when compared with someone who already believes they have all the answers.

Like Albert Einstein I am also curious, but I would disagree with him in stating that he is not gifted as aside from the unbelievable work he did (E=MC2 and so on), I believe that having a curious mind is a gift.

It allows you to ask questions which others do not think to ask, and from there you can gain deeper insight into things which can be of great benefit to both yourself and the company you are working for.

As we come to the close of this chapter, I just want to reinforce the point that it does not matter if you become the world's best interviewee when applying for jobs if then when upon landing the job you do not add value to the company.

You must work hard and be willing to continually learn and grow so you can keep adding value to your employer. If you take the money, make sure you do the work.

Do not judge your performance based on what your colleagues are doing, set your own targets that you expect of yourself and make sure they are challenging.

If you can deliver more value to your company or your customers than all of your competition, you will be rewarded in kind.

FINANCIAL SECURITY

Chapter 6

I n this chapter, I would like to discuss why it is more important than ever before to secure your long-term financial safety.

Mahatma Gandhi once said that poverty is the worst form of violence. I suppose you may disagree with him if a group of thugs had just viciously beat you up, but even still you cannot argue with his sentiment.

Living in poverty is not desirable, and it is an unfortunate reality that poverty levels are rising.

In the UK over the last decade from 2010 to 2020, the number of people using food banks has increased by over 3500% from 26,000 to 1 million but unemployment levels are at a record low as more and more working families have now fallen into the poor bracket.

In fact, a recent study showed that 80% of working adults in the UK live on a pay cheque to pay cheque basis. Therefore, if they found themselves redundant from their employer, they would be in a state of total poverty in under a month with no savings or assets to support them in paying their mortgage or rent payments, utility bills or to buy the food required to sustain them.

The world is in a constant state of change and evolution, but nowhere more so than in the commercial business world. Each year organisations will implement change projects to improve the effectiveness and profit of their business.

There are many ways that companies assess change projects to determine if they should receive the required funding to proceed, but at its core this involves determining if the financial benefits the business would receive upon delivering the project outweigh the financial costs to the business by implementing the project.

There are many methods for determining the cost and benefits of a project, including both tangible and intangible metrics. However, one of the first methodologies used in determining what the projects tangible benefits would be is to assess what the FTE reduction would be upon the successful implementation the project.

The FTE reduction means the financial amount the business would save per annum upon releasing the employees who are no longer required following the delivery of the project.

So, giving an example, let us assume that a company who provides internet services to homes and businesses had an idea for a change project to deliver an automated customer enquiry solution with an estimated cost to deliver the project of £100,000.

One of the first metrics to determine if the project will receive the funding to progress is to assess how many full-time employees the company would no longer require if the business was to implement the project. They would then multiply that number of employees by the annual salary of those employees to calculate the estimated annual saving.

All change projects regardless of the companies industry *(manufacturing, retail, software, you name it)* all use this method whereby one of the first metrics they look for is how to make the business leaner by using as few employees as possible without compromising on the quality of service that the business provides to its customers.

As technology keeps advancing, it is becoming more frequent that we are seeing this happen as increased numbers of workers lose their jobs because of task automation that at one time required full-time human employees.

Now before you think I am going all sci-fi on you when discussing automation let me assure you that when I talk about automation in the workplace and within society, I do not mean a world where we all have robots cleaning the house for us while we are downloading a lasagne to pop into our space oven. Automation is already among us right now.

Large-scale change is a transitional process which occurs in increments over time so sure enough if you could somehow look fifty years ahead into the future from now then the world might appear like something from a sci-fi movie in comparison with the world of today, however, it would not happen overnight and we are already seeing this transition with a more automated future among us.

For example, take when you go to the supermarket you can now scan the items you want and pay for them at the kiosk without the need of the store assistant and while this has not yet made all store assistants redundant it is in the early phases of this transition.

In recent months I recall viewing a photograph of a cameraman sitting on the ledge of a helicopter recording a video from the sky of a road traffic incident for the local news.

However, within the space of just a few years from that photo being taken, both the cameraman and the helicopter pilot are no longer required.

The roles that they once carried out now being performed by drone technology with a high definition camera for recording the video which they attach to the drone.

There are also cars with self-driving technology being used in parts of the world and most online customer support that companies offer comes from artificial intelligence chatbots.

These are just a few examples, but there are so many more.

My point is at one time when people used to hold a job for life, that is no longer the case. Therefore, it is imperative that if you work in an industry that is being replaced by technology at some stage, then you need to make sure you are not one of the 80% of people living pay cheque to pay cheque or you will find yourself in a state of absolute poverty.

When individuals lose positions of employment through advancements in technology, the impact that this has on the economy is two folded.

First, the amount of income tax received by the treasury reduces as there are fewer people in employment paying income tax and second those who once would use the remuneration they would receive from their employer now require state funding just to survive.

Therefore, the comfort of the social safety net provided by the government for those in economic hardship will become harder to access as the demand on the treasury purse increases, but the amount of money going in to the treasury decreases.

This leads to the economy becoming more stretched with cutbacks to public spending and increased taxation required to keep it afloat.

Even now, those who require state benefits are finding increased difficulty in accessing them. In a world where austerity has become the normality with benefit caps, there are many examples of people being forced into work when suffering from severe illnesses.

The application process to access state benefits can take several weeks before the processing completes and in that time, you will not see a penny from the government, so with no savings or secondary residual income you will find yourself in a state of absolute poverty.

As pressure on the economy intensifies, these stories of the sick being forced into employment will continue to make the headlines.

When considering your financial security through a set of long-term lenses, this is also just as concerning.

In my parent's era, it was always said that the best thing for a young person was to get a job and work hard at a company until retirement while paying into the pension scheme so that when you get to retirement age; you have a nice steady income from your pension pot.

This advice continues to get passed down from generation to generation.

Only you can decide how to spend your income or what measures to take in securing your financial future so, by all means, take this generational advice and hand over control to the state or whichever pension company you use hoping they take good care of you, but for me that is a gamble I am just not comfortable taking if I need to rely on it as my only source of income.

If I can make the changes now to secure my long-term financial security, then by the time that I reach retirement age if the goal posts move and the pension scheme has collapsed, at least I will have taken measures to protect myself.

I am not saying that the pension you pay into will not be there for you when you reach retirement as I do not have a crystal ball so I cannot say if it will or it will not, however; the government have already pushed back the retirement age on more than one occasion during my lifetime.

Our government are quick to inform us that there is limited funding for public spending as we have endured through a decade of austerity over the last ten years.

Therefore, if the public purse is already so stretched now, how secure can the pension be for someone in their twenties that will not get to draw a penny from it for another fifty years from now?

Another important consideration we must factor when impact assessing the long-term security of the economy is the increasing population.

Within the UK since the year 1900, there has only been one year in 1976 when the average population decreased as there were 675,526 babies born but 680,799 people who passed away.

That year, however, was the exception to the rule.

Back when my Dad was born in 1945 the population of the UK was around 45 million, however now in 2020 the UK population is at around 68 million.

That is a huge increase over only one lifetime and it will only continue to keep growing year on year.

There are data models which forecast the expected population each year into the future, and they show us that this continued growth will not slow down.

This is not just a concern for the UK, but it is a global issue.

When you combine this with the fact that more people will require support from the state as they lose employment through the continuing advancements in technology and automation it does not take a PHD in economics to see that something at some point will need to give or the economy is due a hard crash.

The only way to be sure of our long-term financial security is to take responsibility for our future by taking action now to protect ourselves.

We need to move away from the traditional mindset that our employer or the state will always have our back.

We need to create a plan of action to reach our financial goals and protect our future, otherwise we are simply crossing our fingers and leaving it to chance.

INVESTING IN ASSETS

Chapter 7

As someone whose hands will tingle and go numb at the mere thought of getting a blood test, if there is one category of television programme that you will not catch me watching, it is a hospital-based soap drama.

As a general rule anyway, I find soap dramas to be intolerable, but in particular I think there should be a special room in hell just for hospital-based soap dramas.

An hour of the most terrible acting and story lines and to top it all off there is blood everywhere. No thanks.

My Mam, however, well she has loved the soaps for as long as I can remember.

First, there was Dallas, but I was too young to remember much of that one. Then there was a one set in Liverpool called Brookside that was so over the top it was hilarious. That one was her favourite. Coronation Street and Emmerdale are another two favourites that she still enjoys watching to this day.

After those you then have a sprinkling of others that she would also watch, but she could take them or leave them. The Bill was a police-based drama while London's Burning was a one with Firemen. The hospital-based soaps like Casualty and ER would also fall into this bracket.

If it was Coronation Street or Emmerdale, my Mam would sit and watch those shows with her full undivided attention, but for the others they would be on in the background while she was doing the ironing.

I remember it was one of those nights when I was still living with my parents and my Mam was doing the ironing with the television on in the background.

I left my bedroom to go to the kitchen so I could make myself a snack. To get to the kitchen, you have to pass through the living room, so I made my way from my bedroom and then sat down for a brief period in the living room to eat my snack.

Casualty was on at the time so I knew I had to be sharp about eating my sandwich or I risked being exposed to something grim like open heart surgery and losing my appetite.

It is funny how things turn out in life as by watching just one brief scene from a television show that I had no interest in, it would trigger a chain reaction in my mind that would have a drastic change on how I would spend the rest of my life.

In the chapter on Financial Security I talked about why it is more important than ever to gain financial safety, however a lot of that information was accidental knowledge that I would later discover after I had already decided that I would invest in financial assets.

I base those reasons on future risks with the economy, however I was not even aware of such risks back on that fateful evening while I was watching casualty.

As I sat down to eat my sandwich, I looked up at the television and could see an elderly patient sat up in a hospital bed. Her loved ones surrounded her, and it was clear she did not have long to live.

Her daughter held onto her hand and the elderly lady with tears running down her face said how she wished she could have more time to spend with her family.

I finished my sandwich and made my way back to my bedroom, but I could not get the dialogue from that scene out of my mind.

How many of us will plead for 'just a little more time' with our loved ones, I wondered?

The terror that we may never get to share another precious moment with the ones we love most before we pass away must be something many of us dread as we reach the end of our roads, I thought.

I did not find the scene itself as powerful as the show may have been hoping for, however the impact of its sentiment carried a punch like a heavyweight boxer.

It placed a magnifying glass over the typical way one would live and on their relationship with family. Perhaps most important, however, it raised the awareness of my mortality and the finite nature of life.

It was not like I was under the illusion that I was immortal until this point. By that stage of my life I had already encountered the death of more family members than any young adult should, however it shone a light on death for a brief enough period that I would question how I wanted to spend the rest of my life.

I have had no burning desire to amass incredible levels of wealth over my lifetime. If I won an obscene amount of money overnight like €150M on the Euro Millions Lottery, I do not deny that I would find it fucking amazing.

At least for a brief period until the novelty of owning a yacht and a private aeroplane wore off, anyway.

It is only natural to prefer wealth over poverty, but regarding wanting to become rich my financial goals have always been a considerable amount more moderate than you might expect.

In the chapter on goal setting, I explained why it is important to not only set your goals but also to know why you want to achieve them.

It was on this evening following that brief scene from Casualty when I discovered what I wanted to achieve in life, but more important why I wanted to achieve it.

Is it not a better approach to spend more time with your loved ones during life rather than praying for more time to spend with them at the end of life, I thought to myself?

In my mind I would walk through the steps I drew out for this little thought experiment.

I first considered how there are twenty-four hours in a day, but that we have a dependency to sleep for around a third of that time.

Therefore, if we are only awake for around sixteen hours a day and we go to work for around eight hours a day, then we will spend around fifty percent of our adult life at work, I determined.

This seemed like the obvious area of opportunity that I should look to exploit.

I then continued with my line of questioning.

If we do not go to work, however, then we cannot pay the bills and we would find ourselves homeless. Therefore, we must still go to work unless we can find a way to receive the necessary income that does not require us to go to work to get it.

How could one achieve such a goal, I questioned?

Being raised in a working-class area and attending a school that provided me with almost zero education meant the concept of doing anything other than getting a regular job had never even been a consideration until this point.

I started to think of ways to generate income while limiting the amount of my time I would need to exchange in return.

The thought of a business with as few regular outgoings as possible seemed the most sensible as my mind started flowing with various ideas.

A large commercial building where local bands could practice was my first idea. I thought about how there would be the initial capital outlay in purchasing the drum kits, speakers and microphones, but after that you would just have the rent and utility costs.

I performed some quick equations in my head and determined this business could bring in revenue of around £300k - £500k per year, however I had no idea what the lease cost of a commercial building like this would be.

This type of business model seemed like a safer option than a business running something like a sandwich shop where you would need to keep restocking the product that you are selling.

It would also be a lot more effort making the sandwiches or buying whatever the product was you sell as apposed to just letting out a space for bands to practice in, I thought.

I would continue to think of other business ideas that only required an initial capital outlay and then minimal time spent working in the business. I remember liking the idea of a storage facility business and also a private car park business.

My absolute favourite idea for this sort of one-off initial outlay business (which did not come until many years later, however) is in renewable energy.

Turbines that are generating power all throughout the night while you are sleeping is the stuff dreams are made from.

Practice rooms are great, but nobody is going to pay you any money to hire a room at 3am for a band session, however if your turbine is generating power to the grid, then you are getting paid while you sleep.

It was exciting having lots of ideas for various businesses and thinking of ways to generate secondary income streams, but it was also overwhelming.

I cannot recall what age I was, but I was still young, somewhere around sixteen or seventeen.

At that point in my life I did not know the first thing about how to run a business, but I knew at that moment that I did not want to work until the standard retirement age and then pray for more time to spend with my kids as I had been too busy during my life.

I will often say to people it does not matter if you are earning £15,000 or £150,000 per year in your job as you are still exchanging your time for money.

As someone who has earned both £15,000 and £150,000 from my employment, I cannot dispute that there are many benefits to earning the larger of the two incomes, however with a large salary alone you still need to exchange your time for money.

The moment that you stop working, that income will also stop.

The only way to ensure you have long-term financial security and thus the ability to spend as much time doing the things you love with the people you love each day is to ensure that you own money generating assets.

Money generating assets are investments that provide you with residual passive income.

You will have no doubt heard of people playing the stock market in this regard. Many will invest into hedge funds or trade commodities on the futures market.

Foreign exchange currency pairs are also commonly traded.

Most trading on the stock markets is automated algorithmic trading these days, but there are many hedge funds and investors that continue to be successful in this arena.

However, it is not something you should start doing if you do not know what you are doing. I keep seeing courses popping up online with titles like, "learn how to make huge money so you can quit your job and become a day trader trading forex!".

I feel for the poor people who get taken in by this stuff. Some snake oil salesman will sell them a dream and a lot of misinformation with a few half-truths and no explanation of the downsides.

Then before they know it, they have gone short on some stock which surges overnight and they end up losing thousands of pounds and crying that this was never explained during the sales pitch.

Personally, I like to invest in property as I understand the intrinsic value of property.

Warren Buffett who has made billions of dollars as a stock market investor once explained we would only make investments in companies where he had determined what the value of the company was.

Then if his valuation of the company was worth more than the price that the shares were selling for he would buy the shares as they offered good value.

He would perform fundamental analysis to assess what all the assets of the company would be worth, the revenue and performance of the company and how they were positioned in the market to determine what he believed the true value of the company share price should be.

I like property as an investment vehicle because it is something people will always need. I have often heard it said before, "you should invest in land, God is not making any more of it!"

There is truth in this as in an open market the price of a product is determined by the demand for the product. So, to give an example, let us say you had one potential customer but one hundred bananas up for sale, those bananas are going to sell cheap as there is far more supply than there is demand.

Now imagine you had one hundred potential customers and only one banana, that banana is going to be one very expensive banana.

The global population is increasing year on year and one thing that people will always need is a home therefore property will always have a high intrinsic value.

Investing in products which people will always have a need for is far less risky than getting swept up by the latest fad.

I actually know a girl whose parents had a business which would be passed down to her when they retired. The girl however did not see running the business as something she wanted to do with her life.

She told her parents this so they sold the business for several million and they all did very well out of it. The business they sold provided funeral services.

It is an unfortunate reality, but a funeral business will never run out of customers as we are not immortal beings.

If you want to invest into a business or a commodity, I would always recommend looking for something that has a greater probability of holding its value as it is something which people will always need.

The majority of people do not actually invest in anything.

For many, they do not even think of money in this way.

They will receive a salary from their employer, and then they determine the total amount of their expenses to pay out such as their rent and utility bills. They then deduct that value from their salary income to determine how much they have left over to spend on themselves.

They will then spend that amount of left-over money on shopping, clothes, nights out, holidays and takeaways and they will continue in this cycle again the following month and so on.

You can most likely relate to this as your own situation, as it is the case for around 80% of working adults.

Rather than thinking of your finances as a single column with your income at the top and your expenses below, I want you to start to think of your finances in two columns.

The first column on the left-hand side is your asset column, and the second column on the right is your liability column. Your current monthly expenses can all go into your liability column.

This will include the essentials like your rent or mortgage, utility bills, council tax, etc. Now add those values together to determine the total amount of money you need each month to cover your essential liabilities.

Next, I want you to determine how much money you need to spend on yourself each month. This will include your shopping, nights out, take-aways etc. Look at your past bank statements to make sure you do not underestimate these figures.

As you did with the essentials, add these items into your liability column. Once you have specified everything you can then calculate the monthly amount, that you require to be free from the dependency on an employer.

Your target now must be to add assets into your asset column that when totalled together are for an amount greater than your total liability amount.

Once you reach that target then you are no longer dependent on having a job to survive and you can leave your employment and start spending more time with your loved ones if this is something you wanted to do.

For each of us this number will vary, but as a general rule somewhere around £3,000 per month should be adequate enough.

A cash-generating asset can be many things and it will not always cost you an arm and a leg to buy it, however in most cases, you will need to spend some money to purchase the asset.

The more money you have to invest the easier it is to reach your financial goal, however do not let having no money put you off.

You can still add to your asset column with minimal funds, but you will just need to use your brain to get creative.

Even if you have lots of money, I would still encourage you to use your brain to think of assets that have the least capital outlay that you can add to your asset column as this reduces your risk exposure.

Your brain is your greatest asset. You can sell everything you own and this includes your home, car, electronics and the clothes off your back and the total value will still be worth far less than your brain.

The ability to earn money from the use of your mind is without limit.

If you have a low-paying job and you want to earn more income, you can learn a new skill and charge more money and there is nothing you cannot learn.

You may wonder what I mean when I say you can use your brain to get creative if you have minimal funds for investing, so I will give you some examples to give you an idea and then you can think of some ideas of your own.

I own several properties, but I also have property that I do not own, but which I manage for the owner.

This kind of property deal does not cost me lots of money to secure like it does when I buy a property. Here is an example of my most recent property deal like this, which I completed.

I provide the owner with the monthly rental price, which we agreed over a long commercial contract for five years.

The property needed work doing to it to make it habitable, but I carried the work out myself. I pay the owner £1,400 per month in rent and I also pay all the bills which then costs me around another £600 per month so my total exposure is £2,000 per month.

If I cannot then let that property out for an amount greater than £2,000 per month, that means the property is not an asset, and it is a liability.

However, I rent that property out on a per room basis for £2,800 per month providing me with a net profit of £800 per month so that makes the property an asset that I include in my asset column.

The property requires very little of my time, and it will continue to provide me with that level of profit for many years ahead. The total financial cost to me to secure that property and bring it up to a high enough standard to let out was £2,900.

Therefore, for less than three grand I secured myself an asset that provides me with £800 per month profit for at least the following five years.

I did not need a large deposit to secure a mortgage or to buy the property, I just paid an entry-level fee for a great cash-generating asset.

How about this book you are reading right now? The capital outlay for this is zero, it is only costing me my time.

Assuming people buy it and I am not wasting my time each month I will get a royalty cheque paying me revenue from the sales of this book.

Is there something you know that others do not, but which people would find valuable?

Perhaps you have a hobby you love which you could monetise by creating a channel on YouTube and uploading videos for people to view where you will receive income each time someone views one of your videos?

YouTube has created many millionaires from people uploading videos that I would have never thought there would have been a demand for.

There are toddlers who open toys and review them that are making £20M per year. Adults that upload videos of themselves just playing video games and yet they have millions of people that watch them playing video games.

All those hits result in revenue and they are now multi-million-aires just from playing video games with their webcam on.

Remember, you only need your asset column to reach around three grand a month, how hard do you think that would be when you put your mind to it?

Put your brain to use now and think of ways to increase your income with a secondary residual income stream, it will amaze you at what you discover once your mind opens up.

These kinds of zero capital outlay investments are great for reducing your financial risk exposure, however their returns are also a lot more unpredictable. This book could be a best seller, but it might not sell a single copy neither.

If you want a higher level of confidence in the expected returns of your assets, then in all likelihood you will need to spend some money to buy those home banker assets, but do not think you cannot invest because you do not have tens of thousands of pounds just sitting around waiting.

Even if you just start investing a few hundred pound a month, anything is better than nothing and the earlier you start the larger the returns will be years down the line as you benefit from the year on year compounded interest.

EMPLOYEE OR ENTREPRENEUR?

Chapter 8

O ne of the most important career questions you will need to ask yourself during your lifetime is if to transition from employee to entrepreneur.

I say transition as while it is possible to go straight from school leaver to business owner in most instances people will have had to get a job first before ever making this consideration.

Only by knowing what you want to achieve in life are you able to determine the things you need to do to achieve them. We will all have different ambitions in life, and we will all define how we measure our personal success in differing ways.

I always encourage entrepreneurship in business because it removes the income limitations you have as an employee. It also adds more value to society as you will create jobs for other people and provide a product or service for people to use which would otherwise not exist.

It surprises me that whenever I have encountered a career advisor whose position it is to help young people decide about their future, they always aim the advice towards joining an organisation rather than creating an organisation of your own.

If you had to sign on for state benefits at the local job centre and they scheduled a meeting for you to attend with their career councillor and you started enquiring about the formation of a limited company and business loans as you wanted to create a business the career councillor would feel lost at sea in unchartered waters.

Get a job is what we are told but never to create jobs.

I have mixed feelings about this. On one hand I would always encourage entrepreneurship, but on the other hand the reality is that most businesses fail.

In my capacity over the years as a business change leader and consultant, I have discovered much about what a business needs to do to become and remain successful. However, for most people this is knowledge that they do not possess and without it they increase the risk of a business they create becoming another statistic of failed start-ups.

I can therefore sympathise with the narrative of parents and career councillors who tell young adults that they should concentrate on getting a job before getting any lofty ideas about becoming an entrepreneur.

However, I have also seen many successful business owners who have started companies with no experience or knowledge of running a business and who have just picked things up along the way.

The reason so many businesses fail is that of a combination of the amount of hard work that is required to run a successful business is extraordinary and that there are so many parts to running a successful business which the start-up does not account for.

In most cases an individual will have a great idea for a product, and they will think this product is so good that the business cannot fail.

Unfortunately, they often find they are in for a crushing reality check as their company joins the landfill of defunct companies whose fantastic products the world never got to enjoy.

Nobody will ever care more about the product that your business creates than yourself. Often entrepreneurs will create a company and spend all of their time working on their product.

They will keep improving the product and they will never stop looking to improve the product, and this is how they will spend most of their time.

A successful business requires much more than just a great product, however.

You need to map out various business processes and create company policies. You need to think about the customer journey and experience. As employees are required to work in your business you need to manage the employees and be compliant with regulations that protect employees and adhere to standards.

You will require software to run your business so you can manage customer enquiries and track orders. You need to learn about tax and accounting and most important of all is you need to persuade customers to buy your product so you must focus most your time on sales and marketing.

When you consider the above, it is easy to see why the most common advice is to just get a job.

If you get a job at a company, someone has already done all those things for you. They have already taken the risk of investing in the machinery to build the products which they sell. They will have already procured the software, and necessary licences required to run the business. The various compliance and legislative regulations needed for employing and managing staff will already be understood as they have their own Human Resources department.

Being an employee is certainly the most straight forward option out of the two.

As an employee you simply turn up and stay for the hours you are required to work for and you carry out the tasks you are required to carry out and then you go home and forget about it until the following morning.

For an entrepreneur who owns their own business they still carry on working long into the night after the employees go home.

There is also no certainty of being financially successful as an entrepreneur.

With a job on the other hand you enter into a contract with your employer so you can be assured that you will earn the amount of money specified upon agreeing to the contract at the end of each month as long as you go to work and do the job you agreed to.

Many entrepreneurs however end up running large debts before the company folds which can result in bankruptcy for the company director, and in the many months leading up to the company folding the entrepreneur may have taken no salary at all.

However, in becoming an entrepreneur and creating your own business you can also earn far more money than you ever dreamed possible as an employee if your business is successful.

You can also vastly reduce the number of hours you actually spend working over a month when the business is established, and you have employed people to carry out the tasks you had initially been doing as a start-up.

You can slowly transition from a process of working in your business to working on your business. What I mean by this is that you work in your business when you perform the day-to-day jobs needed to run your business.

These tasks will take up the majority of your time, leaving very little spare to work on your business. If you leverage other people's time by employing people to do those tasks for a salary that they are happy with and which still allows your business to be profitable, then you can work on the business.

When working on your business you work on the strategy and expansion of the business. You can find more customers as you are no longer burdened by needing to spend all your time servicing your existing customers.

As your company sales keep increasing, you can keep employing more resource until the company is a fully functioning machine that you can step away from should you choose.

Successful business owners can earn far more money than employees of an existing business. I have heard it said to think of a job as an acronym that stand for 'just over broke' as that is the financial situation for most people who have a job.

Becoming an entrepreneur can completely change that, but it can also give you a lot more stress and leave you a lot worse off financially if you are unsuccessful, so do not take the decision lightly.

If you want to start your own company, I would strongly advise you to undergo a course in business management before you spend a penny on the business.

You should learn about lean principles and six sigma techniques so that you can optimise your company's operational activities and learn the necessary skills to determine how successful your business is likely to be based on projected costs and revenues and how to assess demand for your products.

Believe in yourself though, do not be afraid.

If you have passion and you have the knowledge to do it, there is no reason why you cannot create the next big FTSE 100 company.

Almost all those huge companies you see today at one time started off with just a single founder and a big dream.

CONTINUOUS IMPROVEMENT

Chapter 9

TERENCE SLATTERY

I f I have one overarching piece of life advice, it is that we should never stop looking to improve ourselves and adding value in everything we do.

If we care about the work that we do and the companies we do it for we will deliver great work with a high value.

This does not just apply to work, but any business or personal transaction, we should always look for an outcome that benefits more than just ourselves.

I provided an example of a recent property deal I had completed in the chapter on investing in assets. In a deal like that you might wonder, how can you add value?

As that was such a large property, the rent is too high for a typical family to afford to live there. The property was also in a state of disrepair, and it needed a lot of work done to make it habitable.

The owner of the property had no interest in doing the work or managing it, so he expected it would sit empty for some time.

I could transform that run-down property into a nice modern house for working professionals. Each tenant will pay around £400 per month for their rent, but that figure includes all the bills within the price.

That property would cost a single family over £2000 a month

to live there, but for each of the professionals that are now living there they are paying less than a quarter of that amount with the rent ranging between £350 - £450 per room.

They each have a lovely big furnished room which they can lock for additional security. They can also share the communal areas which I furnished to a very high standard.

I put a top of the range smart television in the living room, excellent appliances in the kitchen, and I transformed the bathrooms into stunning rooms that you can relax and get washed in.

I have several professionals all living in harmony and happy that they are living in a nice big house at a very competitive price.

They have made friends with one another and if ever anything in the house requires fixing; I make sure we take it care of when they let me know.

The tenants and the owner feel they are getting good value.

The tenants love the house and for the owner his once dilapidated house now looks fantastic, and he is getting rent that he would otherwise not be getting.

I am also happy as I have a nice healthy margin of profit each month. It is this kind of win / win deal we should always aim for when completing a transaction with someone.

I could just forget about it and count my money not caring for the property or the tenants, but I make sure we look after the property so it remains a nice place to live.

There is a professional cleaning company I have go around once a week to clean the house and when something needs fixing, I make sure it gets taken care of.

When we act ethically and with virtues to those that we do business with and we look to always provide value, we will find that in return money will keep making its way back to us.

If we only focus on making money however and not adding value, the money will in time stop.

As an IT professional, I see it as my moral obligation to always look to keep improving my skills so I can continue to keep adding value to my clients.

We need to be open with ourselves enough to determine our weaknesses so we can put plans in place to improve on them.

This is something I will do by setting myself targets to improve over my areas of weakness.

For example, I have attempted to learn how to code and I have developed programmes in coding languages such as C# and Python while building databases using SQL.

I do not work as a software developer on the projects I am involved in, however by learning how to do the basics, it allows me to appreciate that element of change management better.

I have also identified other areas of weakness where I know I can improve on. The areas I am now improving relate to IT security and networking.

To better understand IT security, I have installed Kali Linux on a secondary hard drive in my home computer.

This is a penetration testing operating system that allows me to learn more about various security exploits and hacks to be aware of, so I perform penetration tests on my computer system at home.

Once I feel I have an adequate level of expertise in IT security, I will then understand networking better. All those firewall rules, ports and tunnels are something which I have a rudimentary knowledge of, but which I can improve.

Never in my time as an IT contractor have my shortcomings in these areas been an issue, but all the same, I know that as an IT Professional I need to keep learning so I can keep providing more and more value to my clients.

An old proverb states, "the more you learn then the more you can earn," and this is very true.

I believe we should set our own standards that we think are acceptable, and then we should strive to better them.

It should not matter what our colleagues are doing or not doing as we should be our own judge when assessing our performance level and if the value we are providing is adequate enough.

We must be critical of ourselves and not allow ourselves to become complacent.

8 STEP PROGRESS PLAN

Chapter 10

A s we approach the end of this book, I want to provide a synopsis that outlines the steps we need to take to start to see great improvements in all areas of our lives.

Step 1 – Stop Wasting Money!

Review your statements to assess your spending habits and determine how much money you spend per month on non-essential material items that you could easily live without.

Acknowledge to yourself that you do not need to buy these things and tell yourself you will no longer waste money on them.

Create a goal to save an amount of money equal to or lower than the sum total of the value from those non-essential items each month and feel pride in your accomplishment as you see yourself achieve this goal month on month.

Step 2 – Be Introspective & Identify Weakness

As Muhammad Ali once quoted, "The man who views the world at 50 the same as he did at 20 has wasted 30 years of his life".

The best way to expand our outward thinking is through inward perspective.

"Be the change you want to see in the world," as Gandhi said.

Personal growth and development will require strength and courage to identify weakness in ourselves and then put a plan in place to improve on those weaknesses.

It is easier to blame others and not accept responsibility, but that is not how we grow in life.

We need to first make a list of all the areas that we need to improve and then we can determine what we need to do to improve on them.

We should all be regularly asking ourselves key questions such as:

1) Am I exercising enough?

2) Am I getting sufficient nutrition from my diet?

3) Am I consuming too many non-nutritious food and drink items which are detrimental to my health and wellbeing?

4) Am I being kind to people I meet and trying to help the people I come into contact with whenever I can?

5) Am I being judgemental of others and allowing negative emotions effect my state of mind and wellbeing?

6) Am I allowing my spending habits on non-essential items create debt and subsequent stress and anxiety in my life?

7) Do I know what I want in life and do I have a plan to achieve it?

8) Am I doing the work required to achieve my dreams or pro-crastinating on them?

9) Am I doing my absolute best or can I improve?

Step 3 – Create Your First Objective Tree

Determine what it is you want in life and why you want to achieve it. Write down this objective and also write down all the reasons why you want to achieve this objective.

Now start to brainstorm what goals you would need to achieve to realise this objective and write them down. Search online for 'How to [insert objective]' and find ideas of the ways you can realise this objective which can help you in defining what goals you need to set.

Under each goal write down the tasks you would need to complete to achieve the goal and make these tasks your 'To Do' list to work from.

Use software like Trello to create yourself a personal Kanban where you can enter your tasks and the goals they correspond to.

Each task appears as a card in a column and you update the status from 'Not Started' to 'In Progress' then 'Complete' with the card moving column each time you progress its status.

Get into a habit of making sure this is the first application you open when you switch on your computer and leave it running so you do not forget to work on the tasks you require in order to meet your goals.

Step 4 – Intelligent Interviewing

Using the interview questions provided document your perfect answers to as many questions as you can.

Use the STAR technique and learn the answers so that you can recite them word for word if you are asked. Keep practising so you do not forget the answers.

Step 5 – Get Promoted

Tell your boss you want a promotion and ask for their support.

If you have a supportive line manager they will work with you to help you achieve your goals by assigning you additional re-sponsibilities so that when you go for a promotion you will have more examples to help you with your examples for the job interview questions.

Then find a position you want and apply for it. Nail the job inter-view by preparing for it like your life depended on it so you have all the answers ready for whatever might be asked of you.

You will no doubt be nervous at the start of the interview regardless of well you prepared, however once you have calmly answered the first couple of questions you will find that you actually start to enjoy the interview process.

Then wait patiently until you find out you have landed the promotion.

Step 6 – Work with Ethics and Virtue

Work for your employer with the same level of commitment as you would if you were working for yourself.

Ask questions to think of ways that you can add more value to the business and always work harder than everyone around you.

Enjoy doing a good job and the feeling of respect you get from those around you as you keep increasing the quality of work you deliver to the company.

Step 7 – Secure Your Financial Future

Create a document with your assets and liabilities and create a plan to add assets to your asset column. Determine the amount of money required to be financially secure from events like sickness and unemployment.

With the additional income you are now earning from your

higher paying job and the money you are saving from no longer wasting on non-essential items you can start to invest in money generating assets that provide you with a passive income.

Step 8 – Keep Adding Value

Finally, I want you to ask yourself two questions before going to sleep each night.

Write these questions down to make sure you have a constant reminder of them.

You could even create a desktop wallpaper with them or print them out and place them next to your bed so you have regular visibility and do not forget to do this. Then every night I want you to ask yourself the following two questions:

1) What am I going to do tomorrow to add as much value as possible to my life and those around me?

2) What do I need to improve on so I can keep providing value to myself and others?

If you can create a habit of asking these two simple questions each night and taking five minutes to reflect on them it will allow you to discover more about yourself than you can imagine.

The benefit it will bring to your life and the lives of those you care about will also be nothing short of unremarkable.

These two simple questions will ensure you always add value through virtue which in return will reward you with increased wealth and mental wellbeing.

ACKNOWLEDGE-MENT

I would like to take this moment to thank you for purchasing this book and reading it until this point.

Over the last couple of weeks I have put everything into the writing and editing of this book, hoping I would create something that you would find valuable and enjoy reading.

Knowing that you have read the book until the end and are now reading this acknowledgement, it makes all that effort worthwhile.

I hope that the information I have provided you with gives you the motivation and assurances to go out into the world and take from it what you deserve.

If you have enjoyed this book, I would love it if you would leave a review and tell me what you found most useful from it.

I would also love to read your stories in the future about how the information in this book has helped you during your life months or even years after reading the book.

If you find you land a big promotion, master your mental well-being or invest in some killer investments as a result of this book, please send me a message to let me know.

It will make me feel great if I know I have been able to help you in your life because of reading this book.

I would also like to take this moment to thank my family who have supported me all throughout my life.

Both my parents who are wonderful and I cannot thank enough. Also, my friends who have helped me during hard times and many of the great colleagues who I have worked with over the years at various organisations as well.

In particular, my fiancé Claire who has supported and stuck with me as I have taken many big daunting and stressful decisions over the years that throw our lives into turmoil just as things are getting settled deserves a special mention.

Between you all you have all made it much easier for me to do the things I have done over the last twenty years, and I am very thankful.

Now for my final piece of advice...

Go out into the world, and leave your mark on it. Know what you are worth and do not let fear stop you from achieving it.

You will get nothing from this world if you do not put yourself out there, but if you go for it, you might just find you can take it all.

AFTERWORD

If you have enjoyed reading this book on your Kindle and found the information helpful can you please click here to leave a review

I rely heavily on reviews in order for my book to be displayed to other customers so thank you so much in advance, I really do appreciate it and the links make the process easy as it only takes a few seconds.

If you have the paperback version you can scan the below QR Code on your mobile phone and that will also take you straight to the review page.

Thank you.

Printed in Great Britain
by Amazon